W9-AHJ-299

BRAINY DAY
ACTIVITIES

Crosswords, Hidden Pictures, and More!

Thinking Kids®
Carson-Dellosa Publishing LLC
Greensboro, North Carolina

Thinking Kids®
An imprint of Carson-Dellosa Publishing LLC
PO Box 35665
Greensboro, NC 27425 USA

Printed in the USA • All rights reserved.
03-224191151

ISBN 978-1-4838-3824-3

TABLE OF CONTENTS

What's the Diff? 7
Rockin' Treasure Hunt 8
Rockin' Treasure Hunt 9
Feelings 10
What's the Diff? 11
Slumber Party! 12
Silly Animals .13
What's Different? 14
What's Different? 15
Tic-Tac-Toe .16
Americanize .17
Secret Code 18
R-R-R-R-R-ING! 19
What's Different? 20
What's Different? 21
Get a Clue! .22
Animal Clues 23
Fishing Treasure Hunt 24
Fishing Treasure Hunt 25
Sunshine 26
Spelling As 27
Beaver Clues 28
Beaver Clues 29
What's the Diff? 30
Animal Clues 31
Pizza Treasure Hunt 32
Pizza Treasure Hunt 33
Animal Match 34
Easy as ABC 35
Bakery Treasure Hunt 36
Bakery Treasure Hunt 37
Nice Hat 38
The Pond at the Park 39
Dinosaur Treasure Hunt 40
Dinosaur Treasure Hunt 41
Sea Turtles 42
Hot Stuff 43
Things That Are Alike 44
What's the Diff? 45
Crossword 46
What's the Diff? 47
Birdhouse Treasure Hunt 48
Birdhouse Treasure Hunt 49
Read All About It 50

What's the Diff? 51
Secret Code 52
Secret Code 53
Zombie Treasure Hunt 54
Zombie Treasure Hunt 55
Being a Friend 56
Crossword 57
What's Different? 58
What's Different? 59
Riddle Time .60
Riddle Time .61
Puker Power .62
Word Magic 63
What's Different? 64
What's Different? 65
Umbrella 66
Mystery Picture 67
Animal Homes 68
What's the Diff? 69
Summer Treasure Hunt 70
Summer Treasure Hunt 71
S Words 72
Butterfly 73
Five Senses .74
Puppy Power 75
Carousel Treasure Hunt 76
Carousel Treasure Hunt 77
Springtime. 78
Winter 79
Baseball Treasure Hunt. 80
Baseball Treasure Hunt 81
Helpful Friends 82
What's the Diff? 83
Library Treasure Hunt 84
Library Treasure Hunt 85
What's the Diff? 86
Around the City 87
What's Different?. 88
What's Different? 89
Weather Watch. 90
At School 91
What's Different? 92
What's Different? 93
Kitten Family 94

TABLE OF CONTENTS

Missing Words 95
What's the Diff? .96
Bookworm 97
Alien Treasure Hunt 98
Alien Treasure Hunt 99
Pig Pen 100
Pig Pen 101
Slumber Party! .102
Scramble 103
Playground Treasure Hunt 104
Playground Treasure Hunt 105
What's the Diff? 106
It's a Mystery 107
What's the Diff? 108
Sweet Spring 109
What's Different? 110
What's Different? 111
Spa Party! 112
Apatosaurus 113
What's the Diff? 114
Fall 115
What's the Diff? 116
Moving to Music 117
What's the Diff? 118
Around the World 119
What's Different? 120
What's Different? 121
Tea Party 122
Mail Call 123
What's the Diff? 124
Making Music 125
Tea Time Treasure 126
Tea Time Treasure 127
Riddle Me This .128
Riddle Me This .129
What's the Diff? 130
Places, Everyone! 131
What's the Diff? 132
Feeling the Sun .133
What's Different? 134
What's Different? 135
Stretch! 136
What's the Diff? 137
Presidents 138

Word Match 139
Cheering Treasure Hunt 140
Cheering Treasure Hunt 141
Birthday Present 142
Secret Word 143
What's the Diff? 144
Career Time 145
Winter Treasure Hunt 146
Winter Treasure Hunt 147
Soooo...Cozy 148
Munchy Attack .149
Awesome Accessories 150
Wheel of Nouns 151
Splashy Treasure Hunt 152
Splashy Treasure Hunt 153
Going Places 154
Summer Fun 155
Word Scramble .156
Word Combos 157
Dragon Treasure Hunt 158
Dragon Treasure Hunt 159
Art Class 160
What's the Diff? 161
What's Different? 162
What's Different? 163
Holidays 164
Calendar Clues .165
Number This! 166
Funny Food Facts 167
What's Different? 168
What's Different? 169
BRRR! 170
Love Day 171
Number This! 172
Home Sweet Home 173
Snorkel Treasure Hunt 174
Snorkel Treasure Hunt 175
Busy Year 176
Happy Birthday .177
What's the Diff? 178
Summer Fun 179
Tree House Treasure Hunt 180
Tree House Treasure Hunt 181
At the Pool 182

TABLE OF CONTENTS

What's the Diff? .183
Rainy Day Treasure Hunt. 184
Rainy Day Treasure Hunt. 185
Kaleodpscope of Letters 186
Picture Clues. 187
What's the Diff? .188
Let's Play 189
What's Different? 190
What's Different? 191
What's the Diff? .192
Wild West 193
What's the Diff? .194
City Zoo 195
What's Different? 196
What's Different? 197
Knock, Knock! 198
What Was the Question? 199
What's the Diff? .200
Space! 201
Equestrian Treasure Hunt 202
Equestrian Treasure Hunt 203
What's the Diff? .204
Toy Store 205
Surprise! 206
City Girl 207
What's Different? 208
What's Different? 209
Bits and Pieces .210
Secret Message 211
Alien Treasure Hunt 212
Alien Treasure Hunt 213
What's the Diff? .214
Rhyme This! 215
Glamorous Glasses 216
Double Duty 217
Barnyard Treasure Hunt 218
Barnyard Treasure Hunt 219
Alike but Different 220
Desert Life 221
Garden Treasure Hunt 222
Garden Treasure Hunt 223
Twin Queens 224
Who or What? 225
What's the Diff? .226
Share Two Letters 227
What's Different? 228
What's Different? 229
Animal Analogies 230
Instrument Chatter 231
Rhyme This! 232
Share Two Letters 233
Surf's Up Treasure Hunt 234
Surf's Up Treasure Hunt 235
Dressing the Part 236
Mystery Picture .237
What's the Diff? .238
Forest Life 239
Volleyball Treasure Hunt 240
Volleyball Treasure Hunt 241
Rhyme Time 242
Nursery Rhymes 243
What's the Diff? .244
Medieval Fairy Tale 245
What's the Diff? .246
Share Two Letters 247
What's the Diff? .248
What a Great Place! 249
What's Different? 250
What's Different? 251
A Rhyme at a Time 252
Unscramble! 253
Summer Fun 254
What's the Diff? .255
Dino Treasure Hunt 256
Dino Treasure Hunt 257
One Becomes Two 258
Grand Canyon .259
What's the Diff? .260
Land and Water 261
What's Different? 262
What's Different? 263
Musical Instruments 264
Musical Instruments 265
What's the Diff? .266
Halloween Fun .267
What's the Diff? .268
Four Square 269
Musical Treasure Hunt 270

TABLE OF CONTENTS

Musical Treasure Hunt 271
Letter Change .272
What's the Diff? 273
What's the Diff? 274
Puzzle Clues 275
Fall Fun Treasure Hunt 276
Fall Fun Treasure Hunt 277
Jumbled Dangers 278
Keys to Spelling 279
What's the Diff? 280
Mystery Word .281
Thrill Ride Treasure Hunt 282
Thrill Ride Treasure Hunt 283
What's the Diff? 284
Change a Letter 285
Space Lingo 286
Space Lingo 287
What's Different? 288
What's Different? 289
Ghost Joke 290
Crack the Code 291
What's the Diff? 292
Picture Clues 293
Victory Treasure Hunt 294
Victory Treasure Hunt 295
Share Two Letters 296
What's the Diff? 297
Goalie Treasure Hunt 298
Goalie Treasure Hunt 299
Letter Change .300
Fun Foods 301
Cute Pets 302
Share Two Letters 303
What's Different? 304
What's Different? 305
Rhyme This! 306
Share Two Letters 307
What's the Diff? 308
Rip-Roaring Rhymes 309
Share Two Letters 310
New Words 311
What's Different? 312
What's Different? 313
For the Birds 314

Super Spring 315
Camp Treasure Hunt 316
Camp Treasure Hunt 317
Picture Clues 318
Picture Clues 319
Puzzle Clues 320
What's the Diff? 321
Lunch Line Treasure Hunt 322
Lunch Line Treasure Hunt 323
Woof! 324
Springtime 325
Luau! 326
Zombies & Vampires 327
Baker Treasure Hunt 328
Baker Treasure Hunt 329
Compound Fun 330
Magnificent Monet 331
Answer Key 332-384

What's the Diff?

One of these things is not like the others.
Can you find the imposter?

ROCKIN' TREASURE HUNT

Find the **31** hidden items in the garage next door.

- ❏ Hockey Stick
- ❏ Top Hat
- ❏ Cherry
- ❏ Candle
- ❏ Leaf
- ❏ Baseball Hat
- ❏ Mushroom
- ❏ Crescent Moon
- ❏ Flag
- ❏ Pine Tree
- ❏ Music Note
- ❏ Flowerpot
- ❏ Sailboat
- ❏ Baseball
- ❏ Lock
- ❏ Fishhook
- ❏ Banana
- ❏ Comb
- ❏ Worm
- ❏ Teacup
- ❏ Diamond
- ❏ Eyeglasses
- ❏ Cane
- ❏ Pizza Slice
- ❏ Paintbrush
- ❏ Pencil
- ❏ Whistle
- ❏ Cup with Straw
- ❏ Domino
- ❏ Book
- ❏ Pushpin

Feelings

Look at the picture clues and use the words in the word box to complete the puzzle.

happy   sad   shy   scared   proud   angry

Across

2.

4.

5.

Down

1.

2.

3.

10

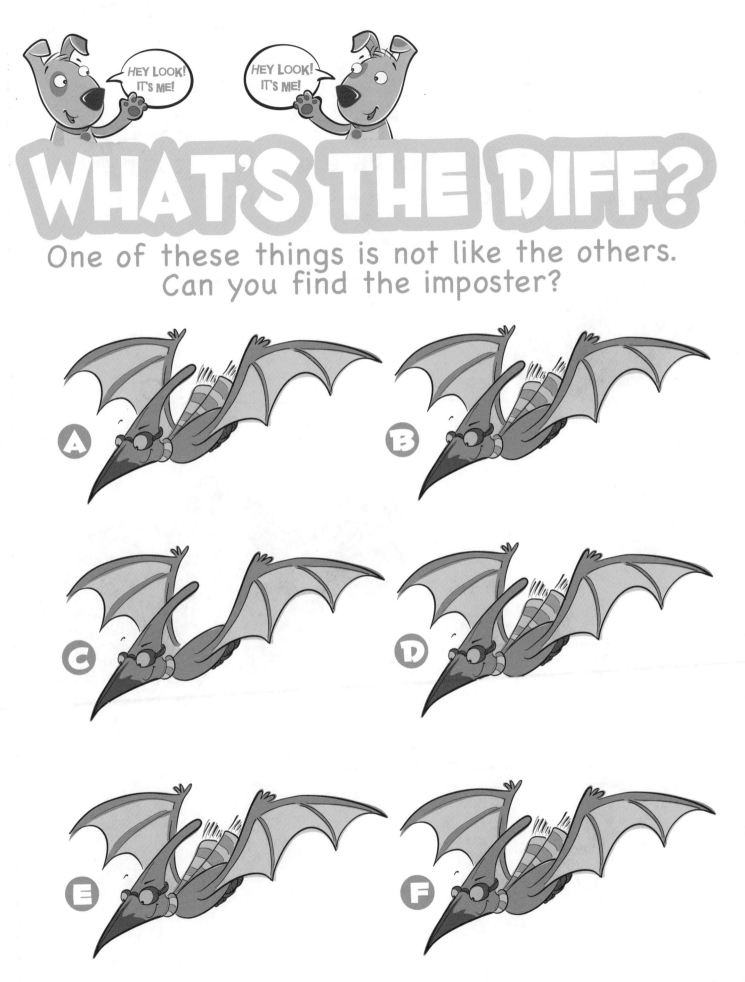

Slumber Party!

Write the missing letters **a**, **e**, **g**, **o**, **m**, or **s** for each word. Use the code at the bottom of the page.

p i l l __ w   f i __ h t

__ __ __ __ i p

d __ n c __

__ __ v i __ __

__ __ k __ o v __ r s

a = ✦   e = ☺   g = ◇

o = ✿   m = ♡   s = ◎

12

SILLY ANIMALS

Below are some silly pictures made from animals put together. Write the names of the two real mammals suggested by the picture.

Then, draw your own silly animal!

1._____   1._____   1._____

2._____   2._____   2._____

What's

Can you spot and circle the

Different?

10 differences in these two pictures?

Tic-Tac-Toe

Connect the words that rhyme with SAT using straight lines.

RAT	MAT	PAT
CAT	WIG	
PIG		
BAT	BED	FAT

How many ways did you connect three words in a row?

AMERICANIZE

Read the sentences below. Use the word bank to find and write the words Americans might use for the Australian expressions in bold.

Word Bank
~~faucets~~
~~trunk~~
~~hood~~
~~gasoline~~

We need to add **petrol** _gasoline_ to the automobile.

The attendant checked under the **bonnet** _trunk_ as I arranged things in the **boot** _hood_ of the car.

Sidney is located near the mouth of a river to provide water for the **taps** _faucets_ .

Secret Code

Write the letter for each symbol. Use the code at the bottom of the page.

What happened when the Easter Bunny told a bunch of silly jokes?

A L L O F
◇ ❀ ❀ ✳ ♡

? H ? E G G S
☺ ◎ ☆ ☆ ⫸ ⫸ 〰

C R A ? ? ? ?
✕ ▨ ◇ ✕ ☺ ☆ ⛊

U P
☀ ||||

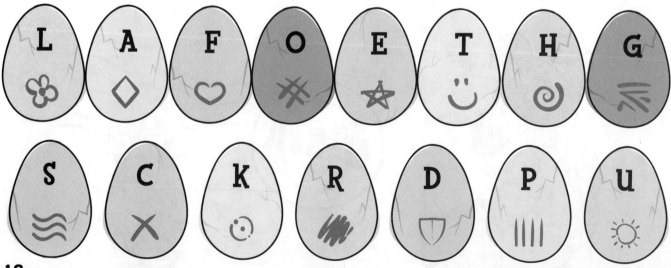

L	A	F	O	E	T	H	G
❀	◇	♡	✳	☆	☺	◎	⫸

S	C	K	R	D	P	U
〰	✕	☺	▨	⛊	||||	☀

18

Use the numbers to decode the sentence below. Remember, for each number you have a choice of three letters.

	ABC	DEF
1	2	3
GHI	JKL	MNO
4	5	6
PRS	TUV	WXY
7	8	9
*	0	#

8 4 3   5 4 2 3 7 8 9

2 3 5 5   7 8 2 6 3 7

3 6 7   3 7 3 3 3 6 6

Use this code system to write a message of your own, and then try it on a friend.

WHAT'S

Can you spot and circle the

DIFFERENT?

11 differences in these two pictures?

Get a Clue!

Use the words from the word box to complete the sentences below. Hint: look at the boxes first to make sure the word will fit.

1. Tommy likes to **play** all d a y .

2. The fish got my **net** w e t .

3. The color of her **bed** is r e d .

4. Kara has **fun** in the s u n .

5. The **boy** had a t o y .

6. Lindsay lost her **small** blue b a l l .

7. Dad's **tie** fell in his p i e .

word box
wet
ball
sun
toy
day
red
pie

CROSSWORD

Read the clues about dinosaurs. Then, complete the puzzle using the words.

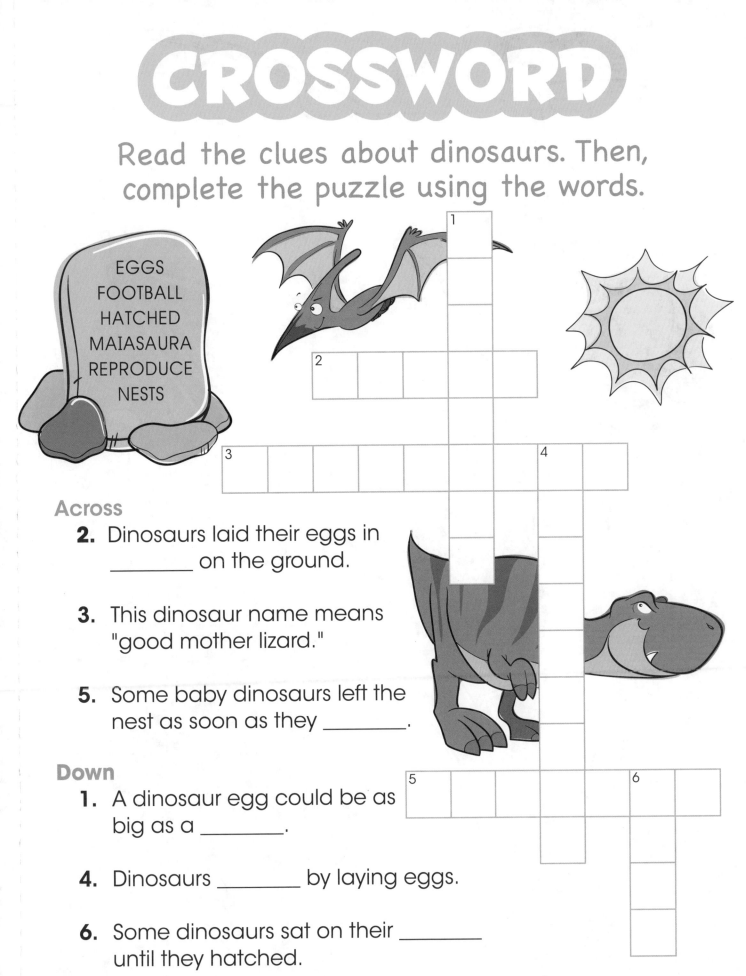

EGGS
FOOTBALL
HATCHED
MAIASAURA
REPRODUCE
NESTS

Across

2. Dinosaurs laid their eggs in _____ on the ground.

3. This dinosaur name means "good mother lizard."

5. Some baby dinosaurs left the nest as soon as they _____.

Down

1. A dinosaur egg could be as big as a _____.

4. Dinosaurs _____ by laying eggs.

6. Some dinosaurs sat on their _____ until they hatched.

FISHING TREASURE HUNT

Find the **20** hidden items in the fishing hole.

- ☑ Lightbulb
- ☑ Heart
- ☑ Donut
- ☑ Teacup
- ☑ Paintbrush
- ☑ Lollipop
- ☑ Spoon
- ☑ Pencil
- ☑ Mushroom
- ☑ Lemon Slice

- ☑ Party Hat
- ☑ Bowl
- ☑ Ice Cream Cone
- ☑ Candy Cane
- ☑ Flag
- ☑ Popsicle
- ☑ Pizza Slice
- ☑ Glass
- ☑ Umbrella
- ☑ Road Cone

Sunshine

How many words can you make from the letters in SUNSHINE?

SUN

_____

_____

_____

_____

_____

_____

_____

_____

HIS

_____

_____

_____

_____

_____

_____

_____

SPELLING AS

Use the clues and the word bank to help you. Write these words like PT would.

A boy named PT likes to take shortcuts when he has a lot to write. He will show U an EZ way to spell. B prepared to B the NV of all your friends. RU ready?

1. A kind of tent   _____

2. An insect   _____

3. A hot drink   _____

4. A vegetable   _____

5. A question word   _____

6. A banana's skin   _____

7. A word that means slippery   _____

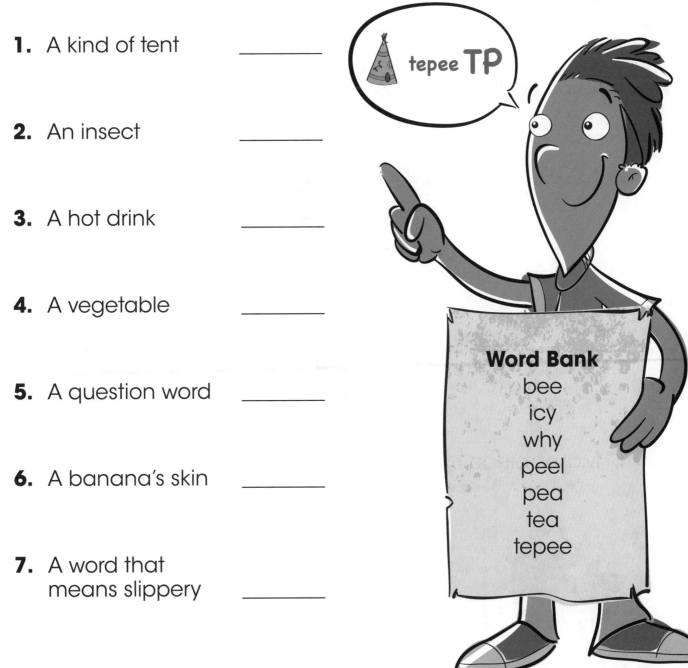

tepee **TP**

Word Bank
bee
icy
why
peel
pea
tea
tepee

BEAVER CLUES

Use the word box to answer each clue in the squares. Then, use your answers to fill in the letters of the riddle on the next page.

a. Lima _____

11	35	32	43

b. To be patient

45	3	6	8

c. Used to chew food

22	41	24	25	2

d. Season

1	39	37	4	12	26

e. Stringed instrument

42	51	29	20	13	16

f. Makes bread rise

19	28	18	17	30

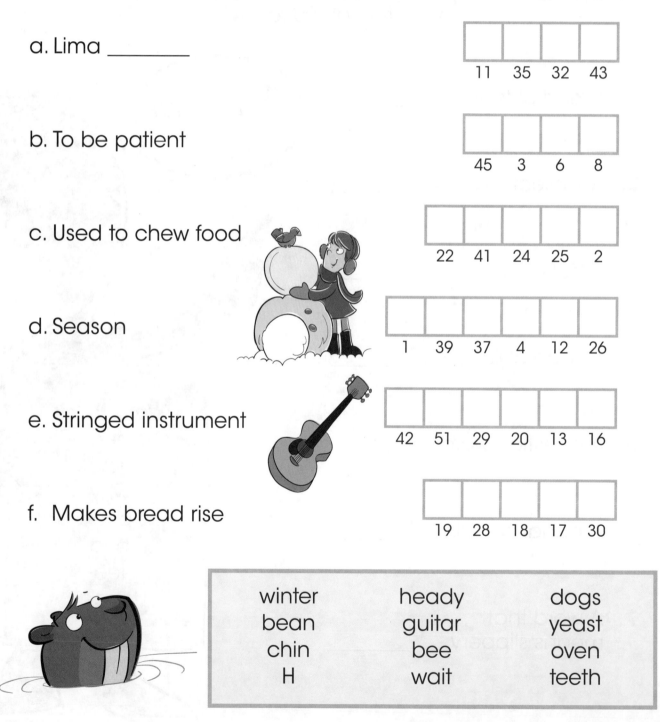

winter	heady	dogs
bean	guitar	yeast
chin	bee	oven
H	wait	teeth

28

g. Wanting one's own way

9	15	44	5	49

h. It's below your lips

40	31	46	38

i. Baking appliance

50	14	10	47

j. It's raining cats and _____

7	21	48	33

k. What insect makes honey?

34	27	36

l. Eighth letter of the alphabet

23

‾	‾	‾	‾		‾	‾	‾		‾	‾	‾		‾	‾	‾	‾	‾	‾
1	2	3	4		5	6	7		8	9	10		11	12	13	14	15	16

‾	‾	‾		‾	‾		‾	‾	‾		‾	‾	‾	‾	?
17	18	19		20	21		22	23	24		25	26	27	28	

‾	‾		‾	‾	‾		‾	‾	‾	‾		‾	‾	‾	‾
29	30		31	32	33		34	35	36	37		38	39	40	41

‾	‾	‾	‾	‾	‾	‾		‾	‾	‾	!
42	43	44	45	46	47	48		49	50	51	

What's the Diff?

One of these things is not like the others.
Can you find the imposter?

ANIMAL CLUES

Read the clues and use the words in the word box to complete the puzzle.

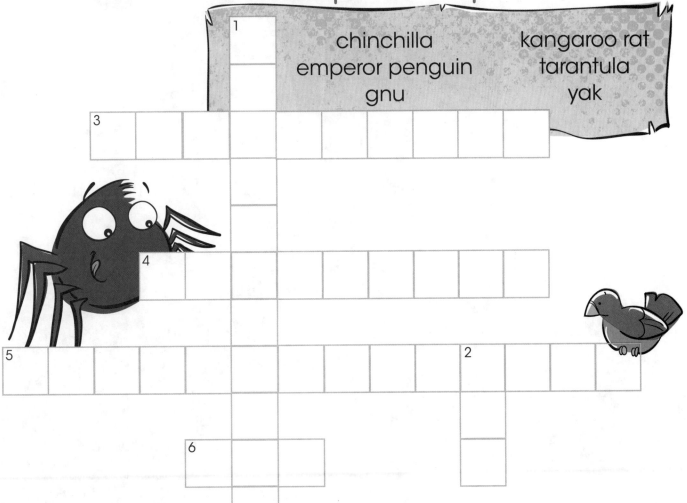

Word box: chinchilla, emperor penguin, gnu, kangaroo rat, tarantula, yak

Down

1. I can save unchewed food in my stomach and later return it to my mouth for a meal.
2. "What's new?" I'm often asked. I only shake my head and smile.

Across

3. While some may desire my coat, I need it more then they.
4. Things may become a bit "hairy" if I crawl near you.
5. Who needs a president when I'm titled for life?
6. I can't talk, although my name may indicate the contrary.

PIZZA TREASURE HUNT

Find the **24** hidden items in the pizza parlor.

- ❑ Lightbulb
- ❑ Bunny Face
- ❑ Peach
- ❑ Crescent Moon
- ❑ Flashlight
- ❑ Flag
- ❑ Cherry
- ❑ Heart
- ❑ Pizza Slice
- ❑ Macaroni
- ❑ Stamp
- ❑ Popsicle
- ❑ Dragonfly
- ❑ Trashcan
- ❑ Golf Club
- ❑ Ring
- ❑ Kite
- ❑ Pear
- ❑ Lollipop
- ❑ Sock
- ❑ Sailboat
- ❑ Feather
- ❑ Worm
- ❑ Ladybug

Animal Match

Draw a line from the animal to its food.

BIRD

CAT

COW

DOG

FISH

BONE

SEED

MILK

HAY

WORM

EASY AS ABC

Use the clues and the word bank to help you write more words like PT would.

tepee **TP**

1. Pass cards to players _____

2. Nothing in it _____

3. A girl's name _____

4. Pep _____

5. I am, he is, you _____ _____

6. A bird that is blue _____

Word Bank

are
empty
energy
Katie
deal
jay

Bakery Treasure Hunt

Find the **35** hidden items in the bakery next door.

- ☐ Ladybug
- ☐ Flower in Pot
- ☐ Ice Cream Cone
- ☐ Trash Can
- ☐ Baseball
- ☐ Log
- ☐ Butterfly
- ☐ Arrow
- ☐ Teacup
- ☐ Crescent Moon
- ☐ Banana
- ☐ Baseball Bat

- ☐ Apple
- ☐ Bell
- ☐ Crown
- ☐ Flute
- ☐ Screw
- ☐ Pear
- ☐ Lightbulb
- ☐ Pencil
- ☐ Candy Cane
- ☐ Snail
- ☐ Pushpin

- ☐ Sun
- ☐ Heart
- ☐ Lollipop
- ☐ Hat
- ☐ Shell
- ☐ Frog
- ☐ Cup with Straw
- ☐ Music Note
- ☐ Toothbrush
- ☐ Dog Bone
- ☐ Candle
- ☐ Worm

NICE HAT

Read the clues and use the words in the word box to complete the puzzle.

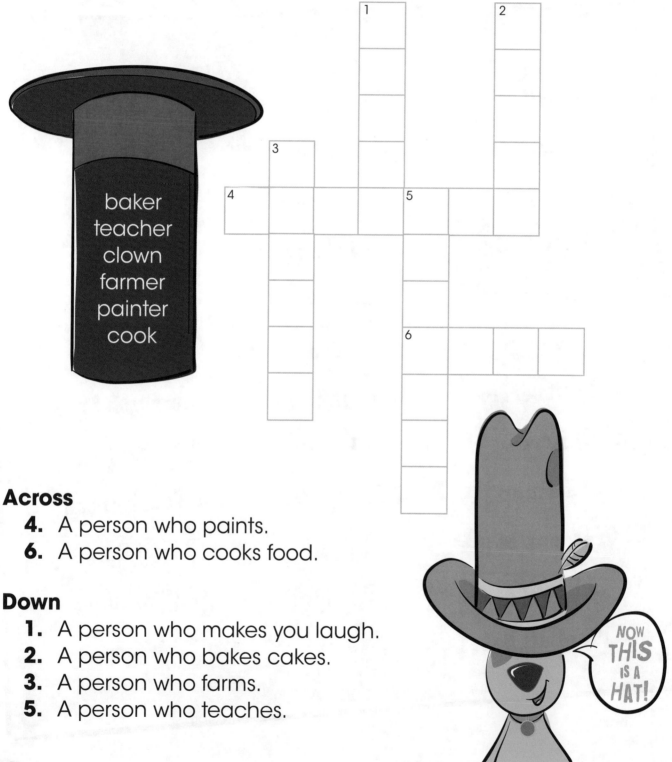

baker
teacher
clown
farmer
painter
cook

Across
   4. A person who paints.
   6. A person who cooks food.

Down
   1. A person who makes you laugh.
   2. A person who bakes cakes.
   3. A person who farms.
   5. A person who teaches.

NOW THIS IS A HAT!

The Pond at the Park

Read the sentences and use the words in the word box to complete the puzzle.

cattails
fish
lily pad
willow
turtle
pond

Across
4. A bullfrog sits on a ____ and croaks a loud song.
5. A family of ducks waddle into the ____ for a swim.
6. A raccoon tries to catch a ____ as it swims by.

Down
1. A ____ sits on a rock in the morning sun.
2. The weeping ____ gives shade to the animals.
3. Birds fly over the many ____ sticking out of the water.

DINOSAUR TREASURE HUNT

Find the **20** hidden items at the campsite next door.

- ☐ Heart
- ☐ Toothbrush
- ☐ Bee
- ☐ Tooth
- ☐ Shuttlecock
- ☐ Mushroom
- ☐ Banana
- ☐ House
- ☐ Cheese
- ☐ Baseball Bat
- ☐ Sailboat
- ☐ Feather
- ☐ Kite
- ☐ Candy Corn
- ☐ Glass
- ☐ Bowl
- ☐ Arrow
- ☐ Mug
- ☐ Paint Can
- ☐ Beach Ball

SEA TURTLES

How many words can you make from the letters in
SEA TURTLES?

TALE

RAT

HOT·STUFF

Each rebus stands for a word listed in the word bank. Help the knight solve the puzzle by writing one word on each line. You will have to respell some words.

1 H + [pot] – P

2 [pepper shaker] + S

3 [hand] – H

4 CH + [shark] – GL + I

5 [onion on fire]

6 [heart steak] – AT

7 [cup of tea] – C

Word Bank
hot
me
peppers
and
up
fire
chili

_____   _____
1   2

_____   _____   _____
3   4   5

_____   _____   **!**
6   7

Things That Are Alike

Read the clues and find the other things from the word box that go with each group to complete the puzzle.

volleyball   spoon

turtle   truck

crayon   turkey

Across

1. pizza   sandwich

3. car   motorcycle

5. basketball   baseball

Down

1. dog   cat

2. knife   fork

4. pencil   marker

Read the clues and use the words in the word box to complete the puzzle.

Across

1. A word you say when you get hurt.
3. A circle is _____.
5. The opposite of quiet.
7. To find out how many, you must _____.

Down

2. Fluffy white object in the sky.
4. Ground wheat that is used in making bread.
7. A sofa.
8. A fish.

I'M GONNA FIND OUT WHAT THIS PUZZLE'S ABOUT!

cloud	trout
loud	flour
ouch	couch
count	round

Birdhouse Treasure Hunt

Find the **25** hidden items in the scene next door.

- ☐ Golf Club
- ☐ Bell
- ☐ Basketball
- ☐ Lollipop
- ☐ Pencil
- ☐ Diamond
- ☐ Open Book
- ☐ Flag
- ☐ Mushroom
- ☐ Feather
- ☐ Popsicle
- ☐ Magnifying Glass

- ☐ Grapes
- ☐ Pizza
- ☐ Caterpillar
- ☐ Leaf
- ☐ Domino
- ☐ Cane
- ☐ Cupcake
- ☐ Cherries
- ☐ Button
- ☐ Peach
- ☐ Ring
- ☐ Egg
- ☐ Sailboat

READ ALL ABOUT IT

Read the clues and use the words in the word box to complete the puzzle.

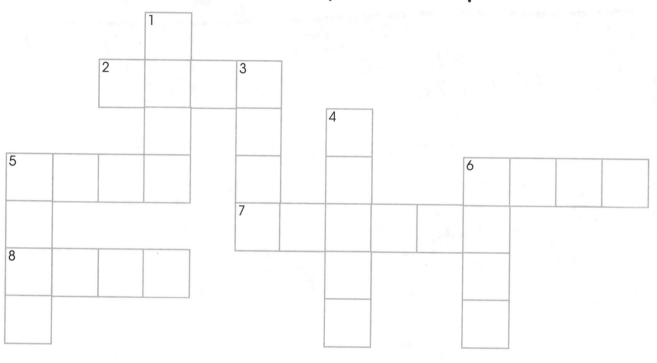

Across

2. To send a letter.
5. Not messy.
6. What you are called.
7. A polite word.
8. Pretty.

Down

1. Used to catch a fish.
3. Jump.
4. To rob.
5. Friendly and kind.
6. Opposite of **far.**

cute   near
mail   bait
neat   leap
name   steal
please   nice

What's the Diff?

One of these things is not like the others.
Can you find the imposter?

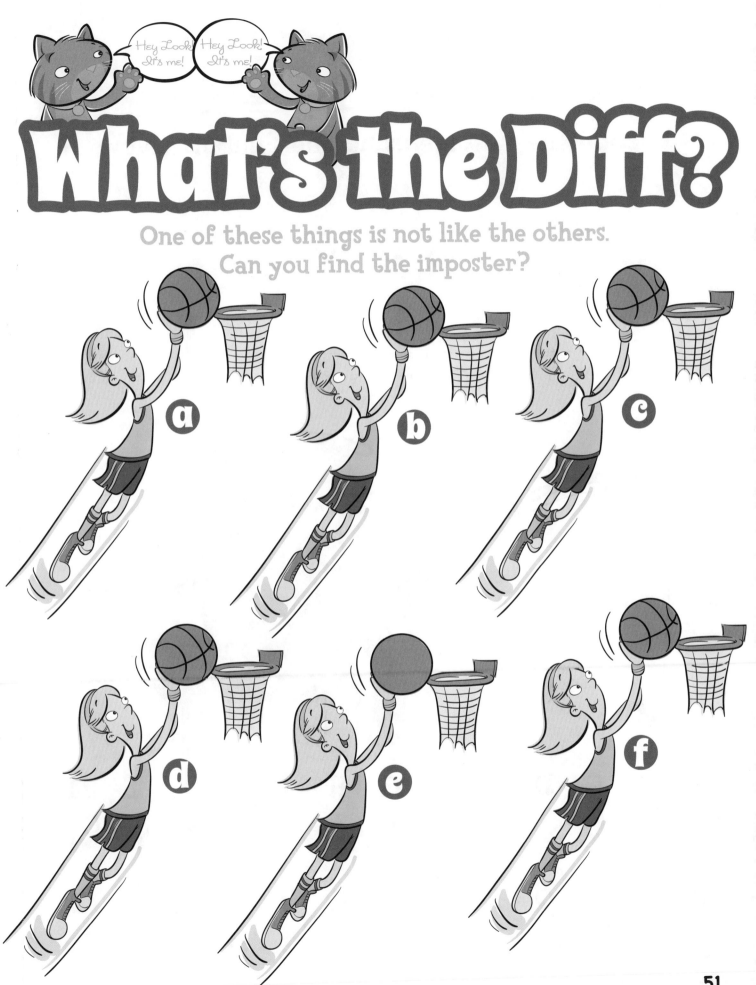

SECRET CODE

Decode the message using the symbols below.

◇ ❀ ※
C A T

♡ ☺ ◉ ★ ☺ ≈ ✗ !
F I S H I N G !

A ❀ B SSS C ◇ D \\ E ∩ F ♡ G ✗ H ★ I ☺ J // K ▽ L ⠂ M ▭

N ≈ O ◉ P |||| Q ▧ R ▽ S ◉ T ※ U ≋ V ☀ W || X △ Y ✗ Z ◎

52

SECRET CODE

Look at the codes below. Use the word bank to help you write what each code means. Then, make up a secret code of your own.

Word Bank

| Twin Snakes | Sunrise | Big Deal |
| Pair of Aces | Too Easy | Sunset |

_____

_____

_____

_____

_____

_____

ZOMBIE TREASURE HUNT

Find the **26** hidden items in the restaurant next door.

- ☐ Candy Corn
- ☐ Party Hat
- ☐ Mitten
- ☐ Candle
- ☐ Sailboat
- ☐ Lollipop
- ☐ Ring
- ☐ Spoon
- ☐ Worm
- ☐ Basketball
- ☐ Lamp
- ☐ Whistle
- ☐ Snail
- ☐ Sock
- ☐ Umbrella
- ☐ Apple
- ☐ Ice Cream Cone
- ☐ Happy Face
- ☐ Mushroom
- ☐ Rabbit
- ☐ Cane
- ☐ Hose
- ☐ Snowman
- ☐ Horseshoe
- ☐ Crescent Moon
- ☐ Macaroni

BEING A FRIEND

Read the clues and use the words in the word box to complete the puzzle.

Across

1. ____ the rules.
4. ____ others' feelings.
6. ____ others.

Down

2. ____ when others are talking.
3. Treat others ____.
5. ____ with others.

respect	share
fairly	follow
help	listen

CROSSWORD

Read the clues and use the words in the word box to complete the puzzle.

I BET YOU'LL BE **ABLE** TO FIGURE THIS OUT!

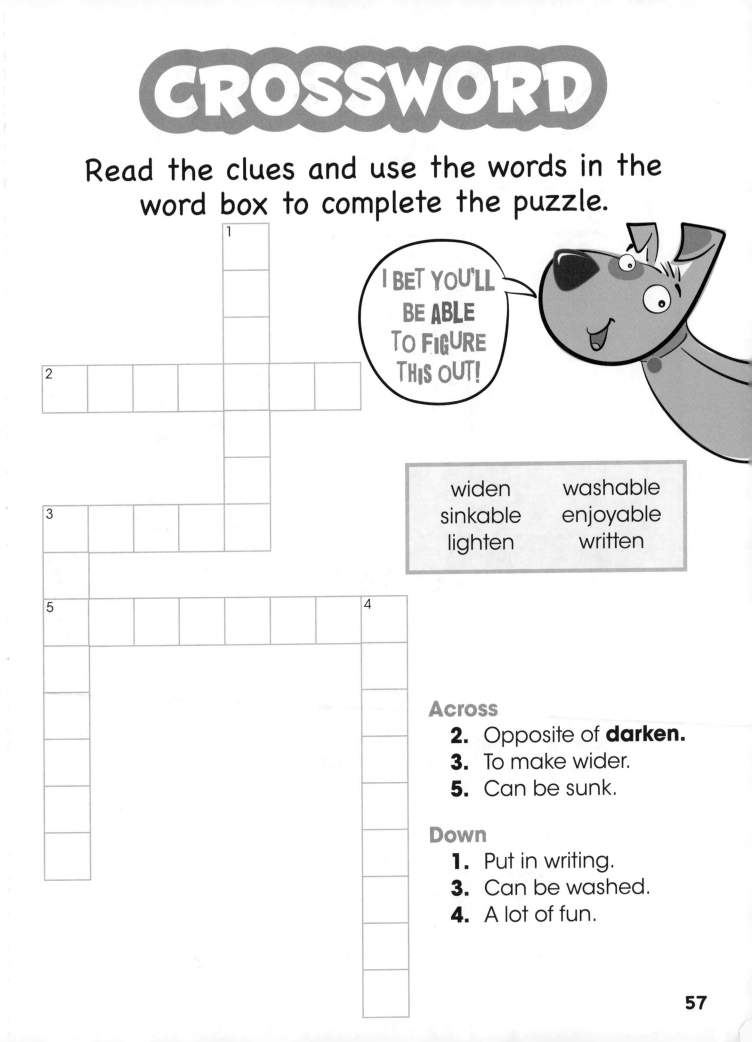

widen	washable
sinkable	enjoyable
lighten	written

Across

  2. Opposite of **darken.**

  3. To make wider.

  5. Can be sunk.

Down

  1. Put in writing.

  3. Can be washed.

  4. A lot of fun.

WHAT'S

Can you spot and circle the

DIFFERENT?

10 differences in these two pictures?

RIDDLE TIME

Use the word box on the next page to answer each clue in the squares on the right. Then, use your answers to fill in the letters of the riddle on the next page.

a. Not old

38	34	40	25	48

b. _____ and thank you

45	42	20	14	32	7

c. Police _____

41	9	24	4	46	11	15

d. Tells the time

1	35	33	13	2

e. You smell with this

19	17	26	22

f. Long stream of water

23	10	21	37	36

g. Female nobility

5	6	31	44	47

h. What you do with a paddle

29	39	27

i. Japanese currency

30	28	12

j. You don't _____? (rhymes with "hay")

8	3	16

k. Second and last vowels in the alphabet, not including "y"

43	18

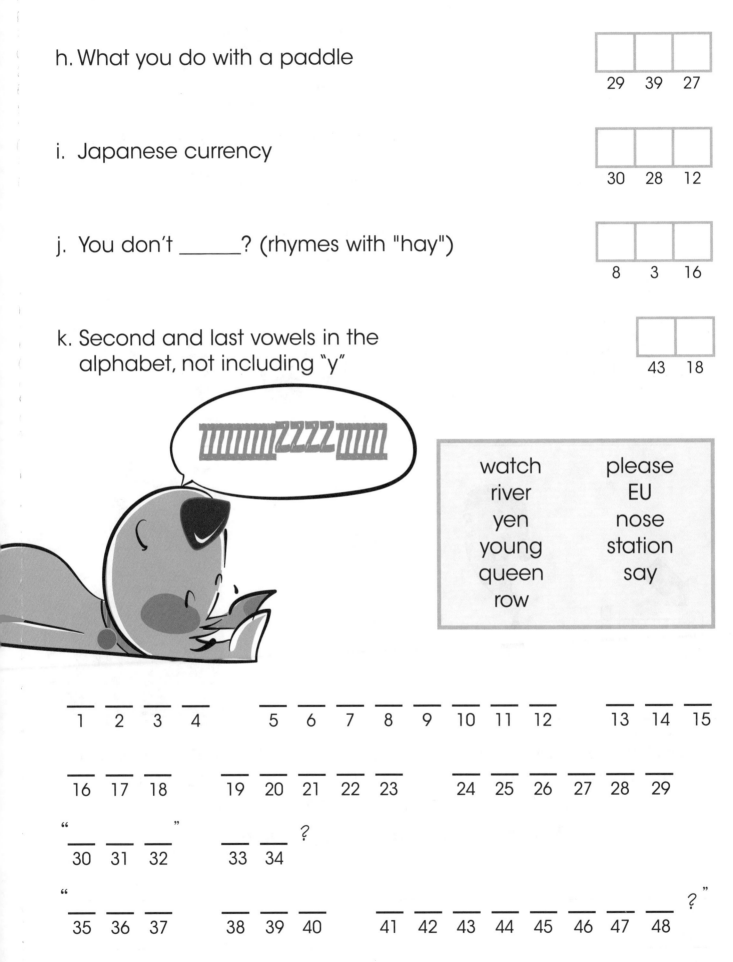

watch	please
river	EU
yen	nose
young	station
queen	say
row	

$\overline{1}$ $\overline{2}$ $\overline{3}$ $\overline{4}$ $\overline{5}$ $\overline{6}$ $\overline{7}$ $\overline{8}$ $\overline{9}$ $\overline{10}$ $\overline{11}$ $\overline{12}$ $\overline{13}$ $\overline{14}$ $\overline{15}$

$\overline{16}$ $\overline{17}$ $\overline{18}$ $\overline{19}$ $\overline{20}$ $\overline{21}$ $\overline{22}$ $\overline{23}$ $\overline{24}$ $\overline{25}$ $\overline{26}$ $\overline{27}$ $\overline{28}$ $\overline{29}$

" $\overline{30}$ $\overline{31}$ $\overline{32}$ " $\overline{33}$ $\overline{34}$?

" $\overline{35}$ $\overline{36}$ $\overline{37}$ $\overline{38}$ $\overline{39}$ $\overline{40}$ $\overline{41}$ $\overline{42}$ $\overline{43}$ $\overline{44}$ $\overline{45}$ $\overline{46}$ $\overline{47}$ $\overline{48}$? "

Pucker Power

On each line, write the word that is pictured.

One day, a princess walked in the forest. She met a bullfrog who croaked loudly, "Every time you kiss me, I will turn into something different. By the seventh kiss, I will have what I need to be your prince."

_____ _____ _____ _____

_____ _____ _____

Each word above makes a compound word when combined with the word before or after it. The last compound word tells what the frog needs to become a prince.

Write the compound words.

_____, _____, _____

_____, _____, _____

WORD MAGIC

Look at each picture below. Use the word bank to help write a compound word for each.

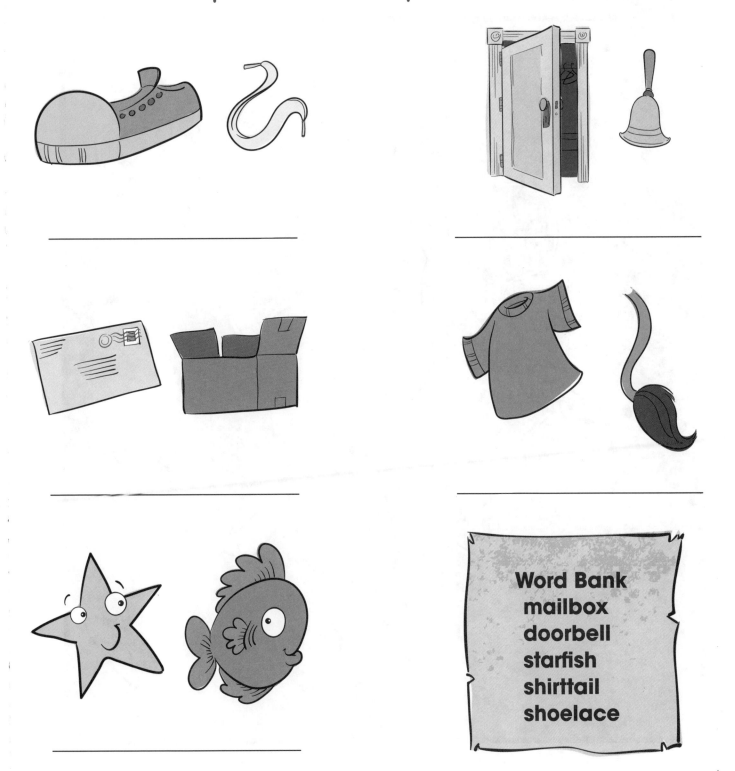

_____

_____

_____

_____

Word Bank
mailbox
doorbell
starfish
shirttail
shoelace

What's

Can you spot and circle the

Different?

10 differences in these two pictures?

UMBRELLA

How many words can you make from the letters in UMBRELLA?

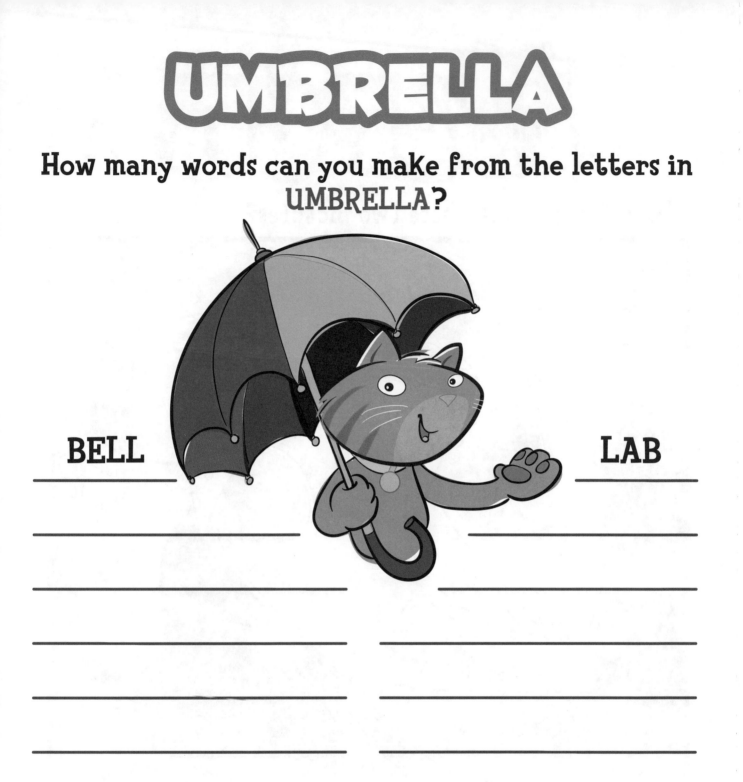

BELL

LAB

MYSTERY PICTURE

Read each sentence and cross out the picture.
What picture is left?

1. It is not Earth.

2. It is not an astronaut.

3. It is not a rocket ship.

4. It is not a helmet.

5. It is not a alien spaceship.

6. It is not a comet.

7. It is not the moon.

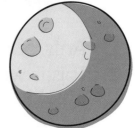

The mystery picture is a _____ .

67

ANIMAL HOMES

Read the clues and use the words in the word box to complete the puzzle.

web
tree
nest
lodge
hive
hill
shell
pond

Across
3. This is where bees make their honey.
4. This is a home for a clam.
6. Fish and frogs live here.
7. A bird makes this home.

Down
1. Ants build one to live in.
2. This is where a spider lives.
5. A beaver builds a dam near this home.
8. A hole in this makes a good home for a squirrel.

What's the Diff?

One of these things is not like the others.
Can you find the imposter?

Summer Treasure huNT

Find the **25** hidden items at the pool party next door.

- ☐ Toothbrush
- ☐ Shamrock
- ☐ Bell
- ☐ Envelope
- ☐ Popsicle
- ☐ Ruler
- ☐ Party Hat
- ☐ Pizza Slice
- ☐ Marker
- ☐ Tea Cup
- ☐ Flashlight
- ☐ Leaf

- ☐ Flag
- ☐ Magnifying Glass
- ☐ Fishhook
- ☐ Mitten
- ☐ Lollipop
- ☐ Kite
- ☐ Candle
- ☐ Ring
- ☐ Baseball Bat
- ☐ Sailboat
- ☐ Mushroom
- ☐ Pencil
- ☐ Umbrella

S WORDS

Read the clues and use the words in the word box to complete the puzzle.

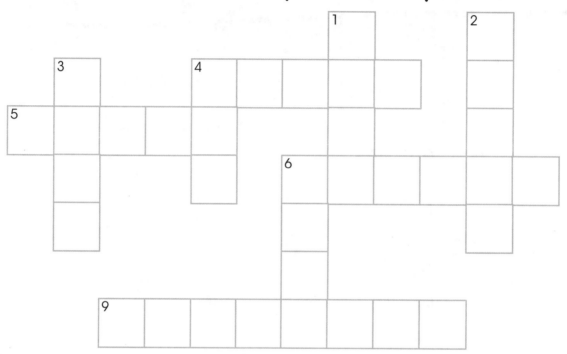

Across

4. Opposite of **frown**
5. A small, slow-moving creature
6. Opposite of **rough**
9. Resting

Down

1. To shut with a bang
2. A smooth, layered rock
3. A cracking sound
4. Very clever, like a fox
6. To trip

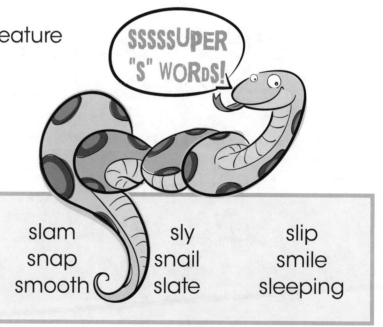

SSSSSUPER "S" WORDS!

slam   sly   slip
snap   snail   smile
smooth   slate   sleeping

BUTTERFLY

How many words can you make from the letters in BUTTERFLY?

FRY

_____

_____

_____

_____

_____

_____

_____

TUB

_____

_____

_____

_____

_____

_____

_____

FIVE SENSES

Read the clues and use the words in the
word box to complete the puzzle.

eyes
hear
ears
taste
mouth
touch
hands
smell

Across

1. Your hands help you do this.
3. You look at a pretty butterfly with these.
5. You use your nose to do this to a flower.
6. You use these to touch a soft kitten.

Down

1. Your mouth helps you do this.
2. Your ears help you do this.
4. You listen to music with these.
7. You taste your favorite fruit with this.

PUPPY POWER

Complete these five sentences. Then, use the words you wrote to answer the question.

Big is to **small** as **day** is to **night**. (Words are opposites.)
Robin is to **bird** as **spaniel** is to **dog**. (Kind of bird; kind of dog)

1. **Here** is to **there** as **then** is to _____ .

2. **Tack** is to **stack** as **pot** is to _____ .

3. **Net** is to **ten** as **saw** is to _____ .

4. **Down** is to **up** as **bottom** is to _____ .

5. **Siamese** is to **cat** as **poodle** is to _____ .

Why was the spotted dog happy?

_____ _____ _____

_____ _____ .

75

Carousel Treasure Hunt

Find the **34** hidden items on the ride next door.

- ☐ Sailboat
- ☐ Apple
- ☐ Heart
- ☐ Paintbrush
- ☐ Dragonfly
- ☐ Diamond
- ☐ Ice Cream Cone
- ☐ Screw
- ☐ Crescent Moon
- ☐ Snail
- ☐ Lollipop
- ☐ Watermelon

- ☐ Key
- ☐ Banana
- ☐ Toothbrush
- ☐ Carrot
- ☐ Snake
- ☐ Sock
- ☐ Envelope
- ☐ Bell
- ☐ Mitten
- ☐ Pizza
- ☐ Button

- ☐ Snowman
- ☐ Donut
- ☐ Bucket
- ☐ Cane
- ☐ Flashlight
- ☐ Pencil
- ☐ Mushroom
- ☐ Leaf
- ☐ Teacup
- ☐ Flowerpot
- ☐ Crayon

SPRINGTIME

Read the clues and use the words in the word box to complete the puzzle.

chick
shower
think
shade
thirteen
white

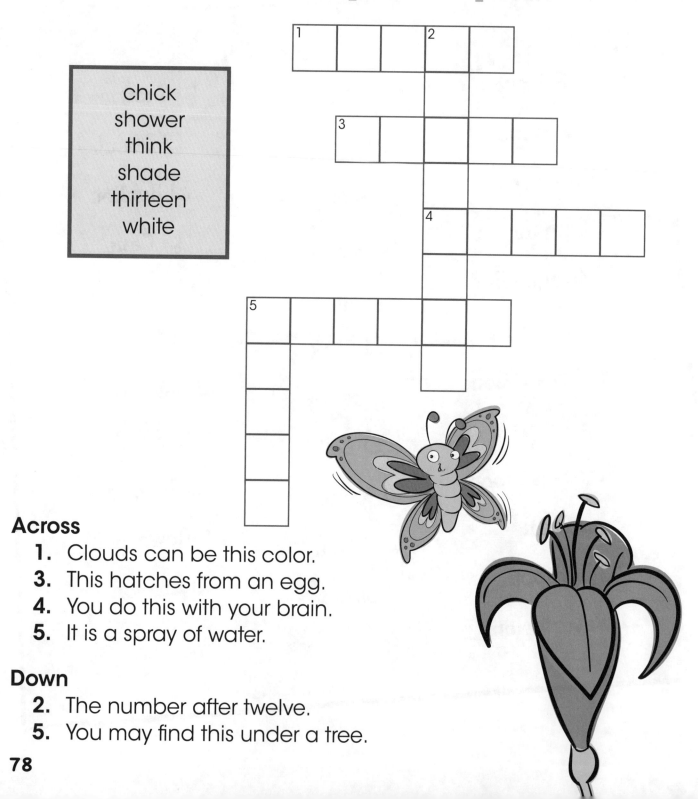

Across

1. Clouds can be this color.
3. This hatches from an egg.
4. You do this with your brain.
5. It is a spray of water.

Down

2. The number after twelve.
5. You may find this under a tree.

WINTER

Read the clues and use the words in the word box to complete the puzzle.

Word box:
snowman
skis
sleep
indoors
shovel

Across
1. This is what some animals do in winter.
2. Use this to take the snow off of sidewalks.
3. This is where to stay warm in a snowstorm.

Down
1. You can build one in the snow.
2. Wear two of them on your feet.

BASEBALL TREASURE HUNT

Find the **24** hidden items in the game next door.

- ☐ Spoon
- ☐ Pizza Slice
- ☐ Boot
- ☐ Pencil
- ☐ Glass
- ☐ Snail
- ☐ Sailboat
- ☐ Chicken Leg
- ☐ Orange Slice
- ☐ Donut
- ☐ Teacup
- ☐ Heart
- ☐ Banana
- ☐ Bowl
- ☐ Pine Tree
- ☐ Ice Cream Cone
- ☐ Bowling Pin
- ☐ Lock
- ☐ Carrot
- ☐ Ruler
- ☐ Hockey Stick
- ☐ Party Hat
- ☐ Music Note
- ☐ Domino

HELPFUL FRIENDS

Read the clues and use the words in the word box to complete the puzzle.

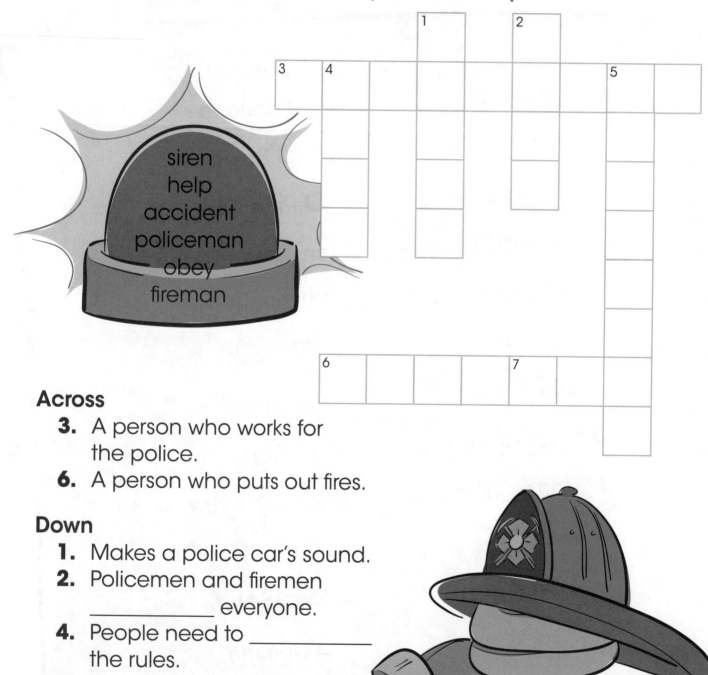

siren
help
accident
policeman
obey
fireman

Across
3. A person who works for the police.
6. A person who puts out fires.

Down
1. Makes a police car's sound.
2. Policemen and firemen _____ everyone.
4. People need to _____ the rules.
5. Police help when there is an _____.

Library Treasure Hunt

Find the **29** hidden items in the library next door.

- Ice Cream Cone
- Mitten
- Ladybug
- House
- Kite
- Sailboat
- Hockey Stick
- Marker
- Comb
- Toothbrush

- Stamp
- Macaroni
- Top Hat
- Umbrella
- Baseball Hat
- Heart
- Carrot
- Music Note
- Lemon

- Trashcan
- Broom
- Soup Can
- Baseball Bat
- Ruler
- Arrow
- Teacup
- Butterfly
- Mushroom
- Apple

What's the Diff?

One of these things is not like the others.
Can you find the imposter?

AROUND THE CITY

Read the clues and use the words in the word box to complete the puzzle.

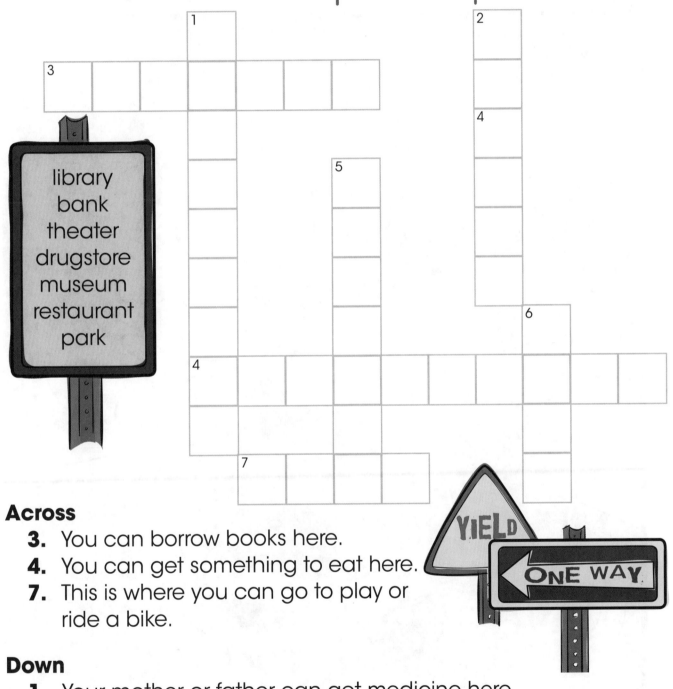

Word Box:
library
bank
theater
drugstore
museum
restaurant
park

Across
3. You can borrow books here.
4. You can get something to eat here.
7. This is where you can go to play or ride a bike.

Down
1. Your mother or father can get medicine here.
2. This building has things about science, antiques, or art.
5. This is where you can see a movie.
6. This is a place where people keep money.

WHAT'S

Can you spot and circle the

DIFFERENT?

10 differences in these two pictures?

WEATHER WATCH

Read the clues and use the words in the word box to complete the puzzle.

rain
thunder
tornado
cloud
storm
lightning
hurricane
fog

Across

1. This is a strong wind with rain or snow.
5. It is a very strong storm with high winds.
7. You might see a puffy white one in the sky.
8. A loud noise after a flash of lightning.

Down

2. This is drops of water falling from the clouds.
3. It is a twisting whirlwind.
4. This is a flash of electricity in the sky.
6. This is a mist close to the ground.

AT SCHOOL

Read the clues and use the words in the word box to complete the puzzle.

teacher
children
computer
read
write
learn

Across
1. This is a machine that helps you learn.
4. You do this with a pencil or a computer.
5. This is a person who helps you learn.

Down
1. These are young people who go to school.
2. This is what you do with a book.
6. This means **to find out about things**.

What's

Can you spot and circle the

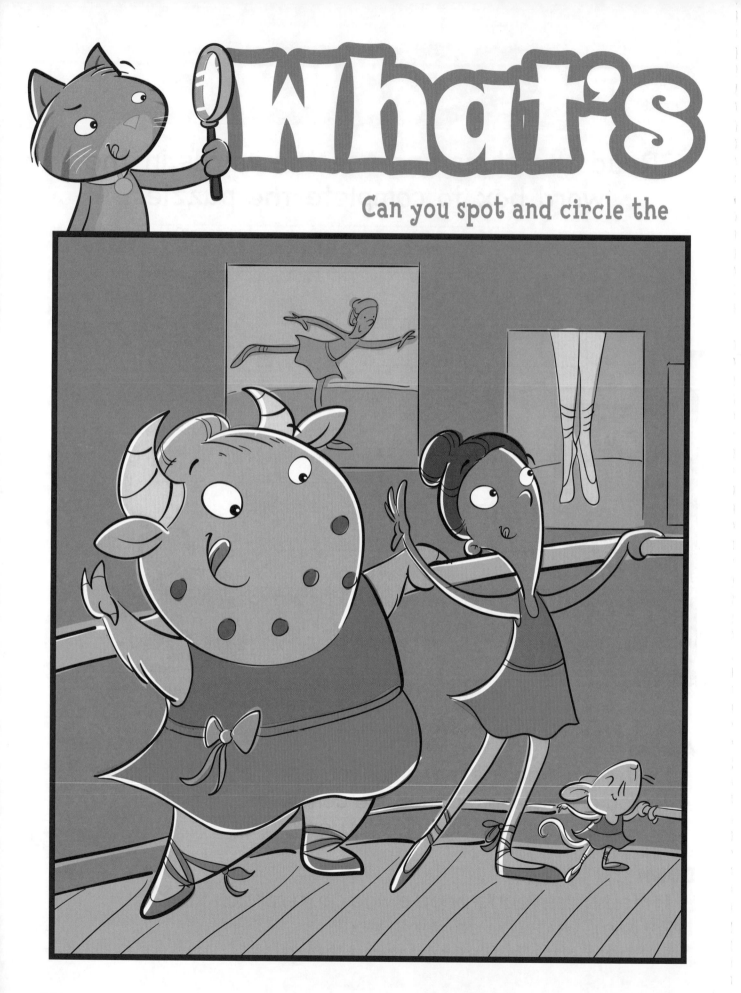

Different?

10 differences in these two pictures?

KITTEN FAMILY

How many words can you make from the letters in
KITTEN FAMILY?

KITE

_____

_____

_____

_____

_____

_____

_____

MAN

_____

_____

_____

_____

_____

_____

_____

MISSING WORDS

Fill in the blanks so the second part of the sentence is related in the same way as the first part of the sentence. The first one has been done for you.

1. **Any** is to **anyone** as _____**what**_____ is to **whatever**.

2. **Come** is to **came** as **do** is to _____ .

3. **Her** is to **she** as **their** is to _____ .

4. **Sang** is to **sing** as **got** is to _____ .

5. **T** is to **then** as **W** is to _____ .

6. **N** is to **M** as **B** is to _____ .

Bookworm

Read the clues and use the words in the word box to complete the puzzle.

title
author
illustrator
date
words
pictures
cover

Across

5. This is a person who draws the pictures.
7. This is the name of the book.
9. The writing in a book.

Down

1. The year the book was made.
2. The drawings or photos in a book.
3. The outside front and back of the book.
4. The person who wrote the book.

ALIEN TREASURE HUNT

Find the **35** hidden items in the grocery store next door.

- ☐ Soccer ball
- ☐ Balloon
- ☐ Lightning Bolt
- ☐ Spoon
- ☐ Teepee
- ☐ Hat
- ☐ Book
- ☐ Boot
- ☐ Envelope
- ☐ Button
- ☐ Hockey Stick
- ☐ Kite
- ☐ Cane
- ☐ Lamp
- ☐ Snowman
- ☐ Eyeglasses
- ☐ Ring
- ☐ Music Note
- ☐ Donut
- ☐ Stamp
- ☐ Pencil
- ☐ Ruler
- ☐ Flag
- ☐ Banana
- ☐ Paintbrush
- ☐ Peach
- ☐ Happy Face
- ☐ Candle
- ☐ Hammer
- ☐ Popcorn Bucket
- ☐ Crown
- ☐ Trash Can
- ☐ Heart
- ☐ Cup with Straw
- ☐ Arrow

PIG PEN

Use the word box to answer each clue in the squares. Then, use your answers to fill in the letters of the riddle on the next page.

a. Makes you say, "Ouch!"

8	3	9	12

b. Class where you learn to add

25	11	4	32

c. Where bees live

17	14	19	41

d. Hospital room with a TV and magazines

1	7	21	31	34	42	10

e. You bake in it

30	35	20	22

29	18	38	16

f. Piggy _____

g. Swimming place

40	24	27	33

h. Opposite of "subtract"

39	5	13

i. It lays eggs

2	36	28

j. A penny is a _____

23	6	37	15

k. Thirteenth letter of the alphabet

26

coin   hen
hive   math
bank   M
pain   add
pool   waiting
oven

$\overline{\quad}_1\ \overline{\quad}_2\ \overline{\quad}_3\ \overline{\quad}_4\quad \overline{\quad}_5\ \overline{\quad}_6\quad \overline{\quad}_7\quad \overline{\quad}_8\ \overline{\quad}_9\ \overline{\quad}_{10}\quad \overline{\quad}_{11}\ \overline{\quad}_{12}\ \overline{\quad}_{13}$

1   2   3   4   5   6   7   8   9   10   11   12   13

_____ ?

14 15 16   17 18 19 20   21 22   23 24 25 26 27 28

_____ .

29 30 31 32   33 34 35 36   37 38   39   40 41 42

Slumber Party!

Unscramble the words and write them on the lines.

wlpiol ___ ___ ___ ___ ___ ___

sgpios ___ ___ ___ ___ ___ ___

mgeas ___ ___ ___ ___ ___

vsoiem ___ ___ ___ ___ ___ ___

esligpen agb

___ ___ ___ ___ ___ ___ ___ ___ ___ ___ ___

SCRAMBLE

Use the words in the word bank to write the missing words in the sentences. Then, unscramble the letters in the circles to find out what Stegosaurus liked to eat.

Stegosaurus had a small ___ ___ (a) ___ .

Stegosaurus had sharp ___ (p) ___ ___ ___ ___ on the end of its tail.

Stegosaurus was about 25 ___ ___ ___ (t) long.

Stegosaurus weighed over 3 ___ ___ ___ (s) .

Stegosaurus had bony ___ (l) ___ ___ ___ ___ on its back.

Its head was close to the ___ ___ ___ ___ (n) ___ .

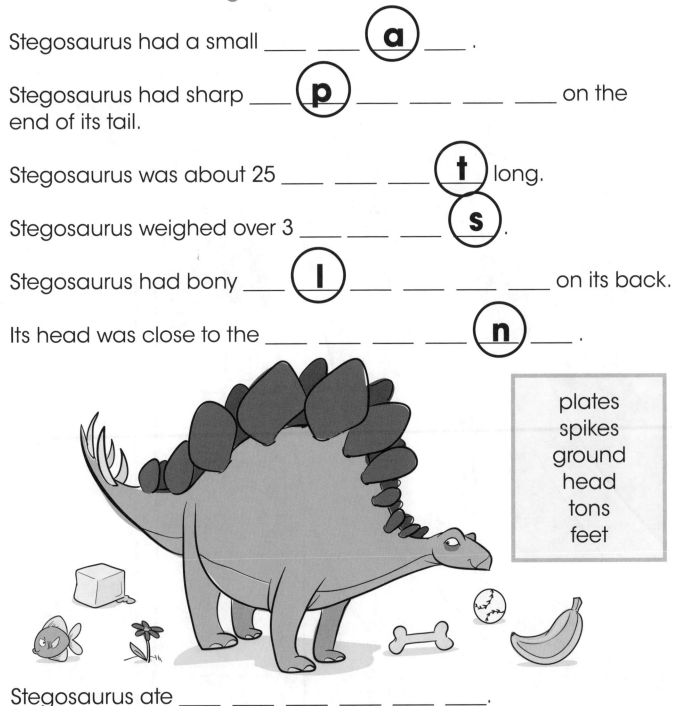

plates
spikes
ground
head
tons
feet

Stegosaurus ate ___ ___ ___ ___ ___ ___ .

Playground Treasure Hunt

Find the **25** hidden items on the playground next door.

- [ ] Butterfly
- [ ] Fork
- [ ] Flag
- [ ] Baseball Bat
- [ ] Fishhook
- [ ] Leaf
- [ ] Candy Corn
- [ ] Rabbit
- [ ] Heart
- [ ] Rainbow
- [ ] Ice Cream Cone
- [ ] Donut
- [ ] Bell
- [ ] Kite
- [ ] Mushroom
- [ ] Sailboat
- [ ] Flashlight
- [ ] Music Note
- [ ] Lollipop
- [ ] Mitten
- [ ] Bowl
- [ ] Spoon
- [ ] Popsicle
- [ ] Toothbrush
- [ ] Party Hat

WHAT'S THE DIFF?

One of these things is not like the others.
Can you find the imposter?

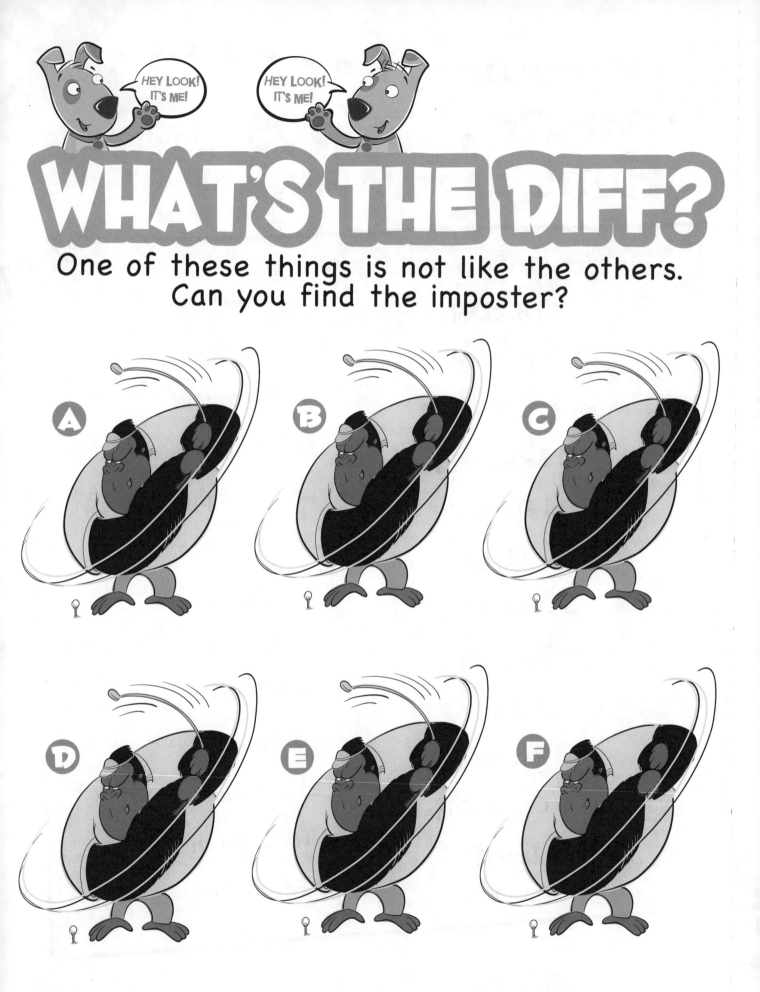

Fill in the puzzle with the words that name the pictures below. Use the word box to help you.

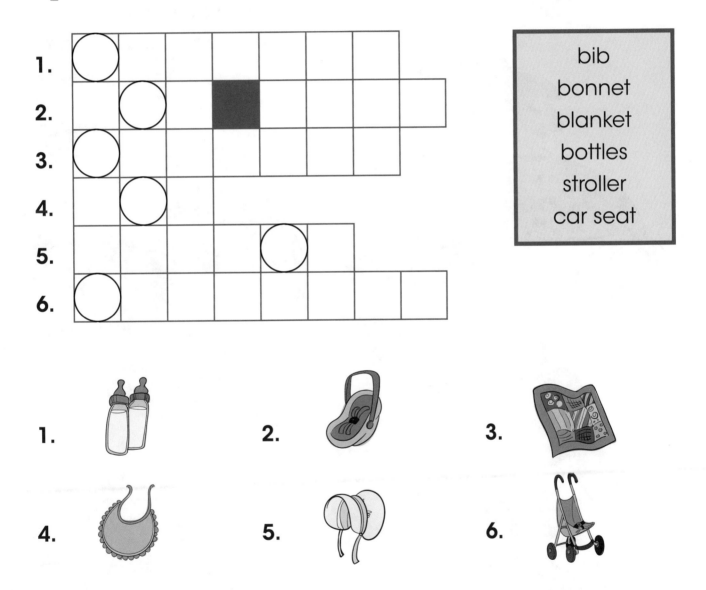

bib
bonnet
blanket
bottles
stroller
car seat

1.

2.

3.

4.

5.

6.

The letters in the circles going down the puzzle spell a mystery word. The word names people who might use all these items. Write the mystery word.

_____

108

Sweet Spring

Read the clues and use the words in the word box to complete the puzzle.

warmer
flowers
caterpillar
windy
rainy
kite
outdoors

Across

2. It is the opposite of **colder**.
3. These bloom in the spring.
6. You can fly one outdoors in the spring.
7. Take your umbrella on days like this.

Down

1. This is busy eating new leaves in spring.
4. It's fun to play here.
5. This is a good day to fly a kite.

What's

Can you spot and circle the

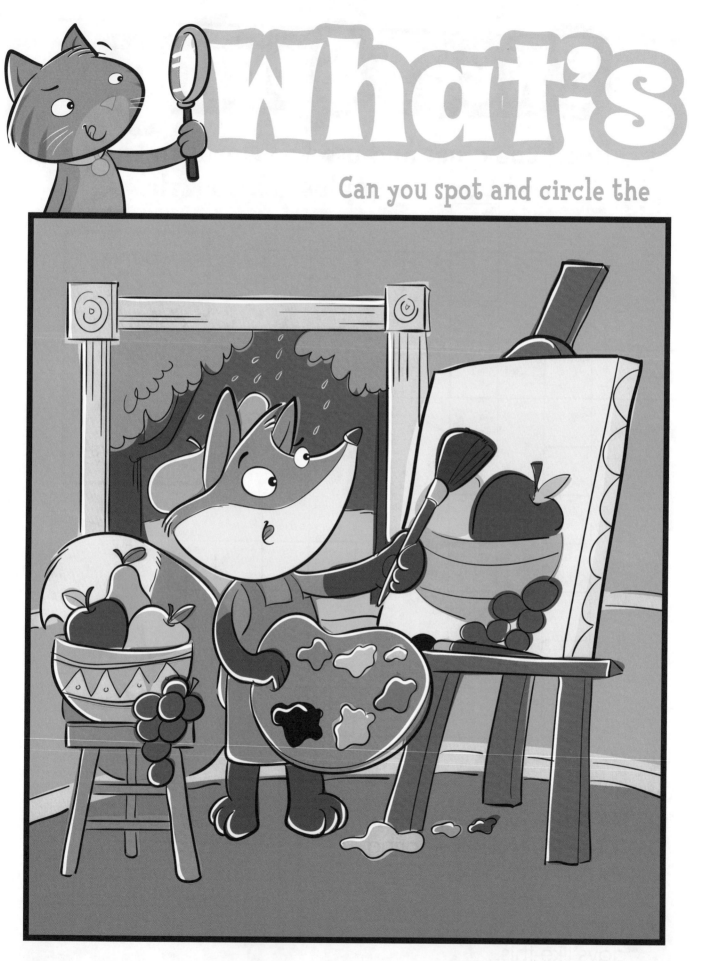

10 differences in these two pictures?

Spa Party!

Unscramble the words and write them on the lines.

nrmeacui __ __ __ __ __ __ __ __

varkmeoe __ __ __ __ __ __ __ __

deipurce __ __ __ __ __ __ __ __

filaca __ __ __ __ __ __

smasega __ __ __ __ __ __ __

APATOSAURUS

Create a rhyme about Apatosaurus. Fill in each blank using the information given.

Its neck was long.

Its bones were ___ ___ ___ ___ ___ ___.

It reached with ease to the tops of ___ ___ ___ ___ ___.

Its skin was ___ ___ ___ ___ ___.

And that's enough!

113

WHAT'S THE DIFF?

One of these things is not like the others.
Can you find the imposter?

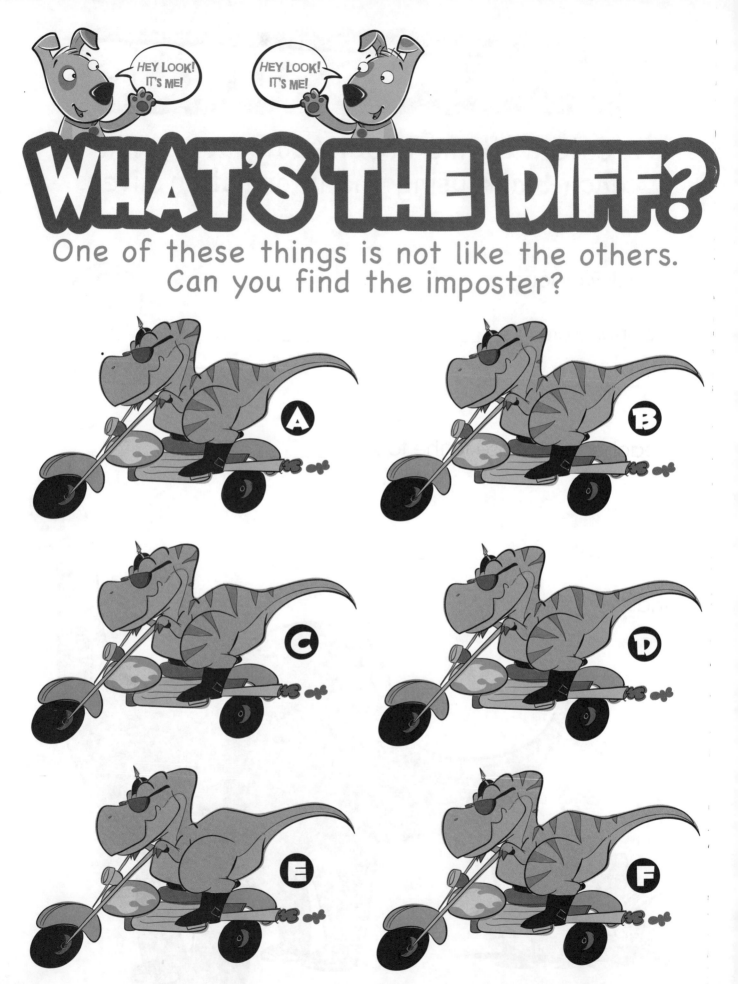

FALL

Read the clues and use the words in the word box to complete the puzzle.

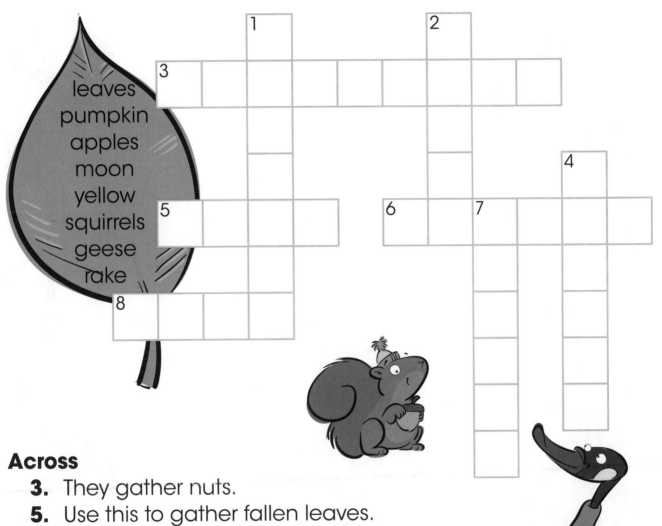

Word box (on leaf):
- leaves
- pumpkin
- apples
- moon
- yellow
- squirrels
- geese
- rake

Across
3. They gather nuts.
5. Use this to gather fallen leaves.
6. These change color in the fall.
8. This looks big and bright in the sky.

Down
1. Pick a big, orange one.
2. They fly south in the fall.
4. Leaves turn red, brown, and this color.
7. Pick a basket of red, ripe ones.

What's the Diff?

One of these things is not like the others.
Can you find the imposter?

Moving to Music

Read the clues and use the words in the word box to complete the puzzle.

stretch	step
dance	skip
leap	whirl
glide	pose

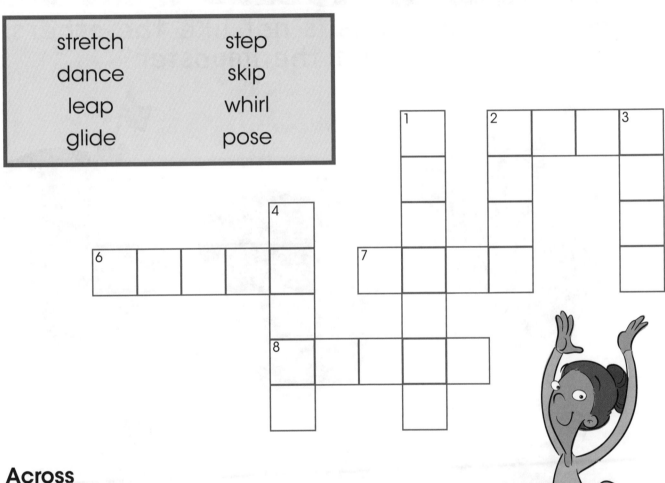

Across
2. This is another word for **walk**.
6. You turn fast when you do this.
7. It is a jump.
8. You do this when you move to music.

Down
1. Reach out and make your body fill more space.
2. You do this when you move with little leaps.
3. You do this when you stand very still.
4. This means **moving smoothly**.

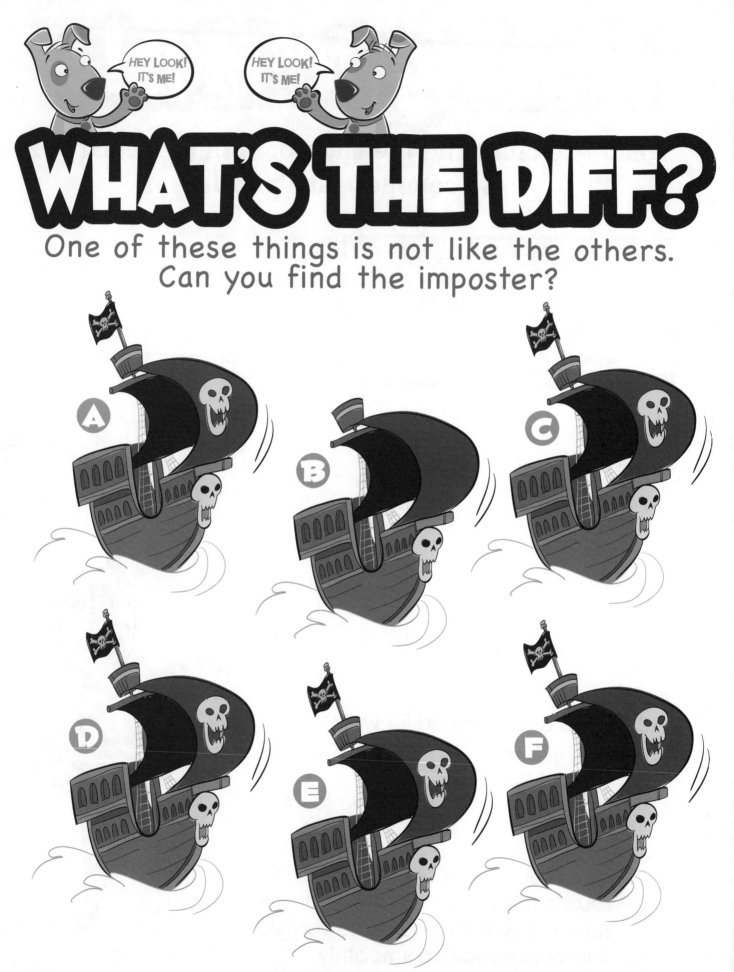

Read the clues and use the words in the word box to complete the puzzle.

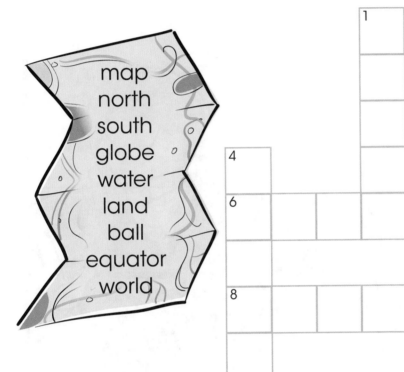

map
north
south
globe
water
land
ball
equator
world

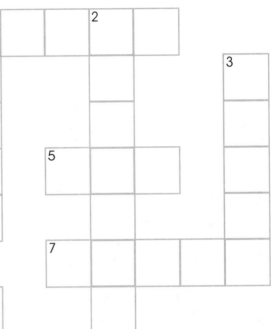

Across
1. It is blue on a globe.
5. It is a drawing of land and water on Earth.
6. It is green on a globe.
7. This is the direction moving toward the bottom of the globe.
8. A globe is shaped like a _____.

Down
1. A globe is a map of this.
2. It is an imaginary line around the middle of Earth.
3. The direction moving toward the top of the globe.
4. It is a model of Earth that is shaped like a ball.

WHAT'S

Can you spot and circle the

DIFFERENT?

10 differences in these two pictures?

Tea Party

Unscramble the words and write them on the lines.

etopat __ __ __ __ __ __

eta pcu __ __ __   __ __ __

mcerear __ __ __ __ __ __ __

gsaru __ __ __ __ __

nsceo __ __ __ __ __

MAIL CALL

Unscramble the words that have to do with mail. Use the words in the word bank to help you.

rettles __ __ __ __ __ __ __

cpageksa __ __ __ __ __ __ __ __

axombli __ __ __ __ __ __ __

leeydivr __ __ __ __ __ __ __ __

dracs __ __ __ __ __

delivery

letters

mailbox

cards

packages

Draw a picture of your favorite thing to receive in the mail.

WHAT'S THE DIFF?

One of these things is not like the others.
Can you find the imposter?

124

Making Music

Read the clues and use the words in the word box to complete the puzzle.

drum
horn
violin
piano
guitar
note
music
listen

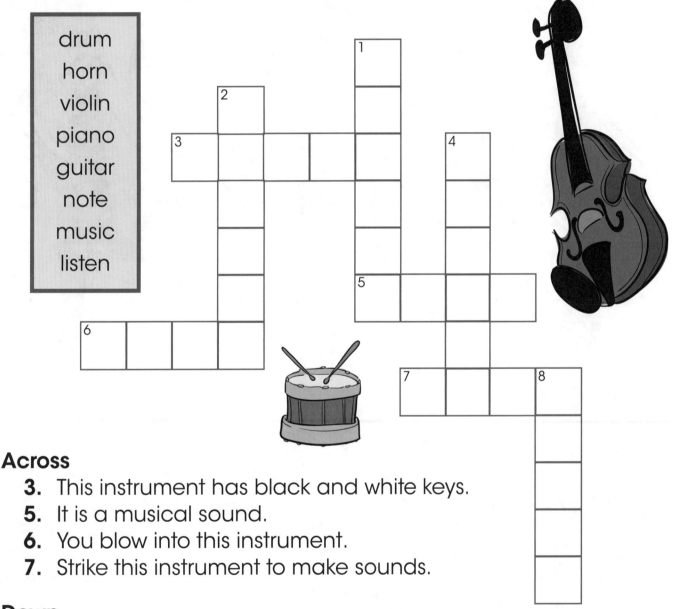

Across
3. This instrument has black and white keys.
5. It is a musical sound.
6. You blow into this instrument.
7. Strike this instrument to make sounds.

Down
1. You play the strings on this instrument with a bow.
2. People do this when they hear music.
4. An electric one is used for rock and roll.
8. It is another word for **beautiful sounds**.

Tea Time Treasure Hunt

Find the **24** hidden items at the party next door.

- ☐ Spoon
- ☐ Lemon Slice
- ☐ Pennant
- ☐ Turtle
- ☐ Crescent Moon
- ☐ Mitten
- ☐ Cinnamon Bun
- ☐ Heart
- ☐ Kite
- ☐ Butterfly
- ☐ Crown
- ☐ Cane

- ☐ Bell
- ☐ Whale
- ☐ Music Note
- ☐ Toothbrush
- ☐ Bird
- ☐ Pizza
- ☐ Fishhook
- ☐ Lollipop
- ☐ Snail
- ☐ Paintbrush
- ☐ Field Hockey Stick
- ☐ Banana

RIDDLE ME THIS

Use the word box on the next page to answer each clue in the squares. Then, use your answers to fill in the letters of the riddle on the next page.

a. Above your eyebrows

24	12	7	21	17	14	3	8

b. Keeps time on your wrist

1	28	37	11	2

c. Piece of clothing

16	46	43	39	31

d. Danger; rhymes with "bubble"

20	19	6	27	9	34	35

e. Breed of dog; Irish _____

45	10	36	4	38	22

f. Used to make a fire

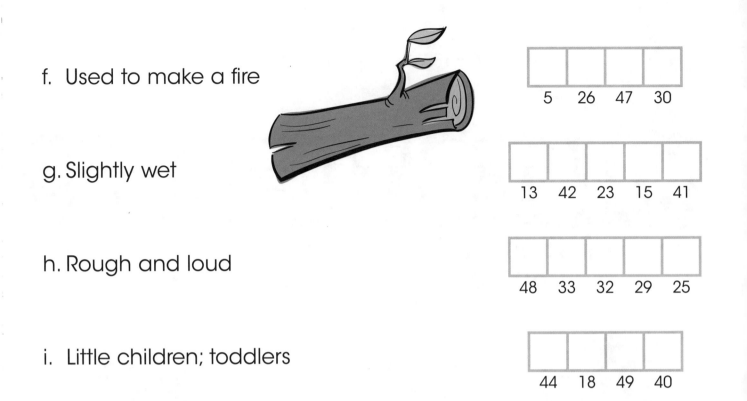

5	26	47	30

g. Slightly wet

13	42	23	15	41

h. Rough and loud

48	33	32	29	25

i. Little children; toddlers

44	18	49	40

trouble	tots
rowdy	forehead
watch	moist
wood	shirt
setter	

$\overline{}$ $\overline{}$ $\overline{}$ $\overline{}$ $\overline{}$ $\overline{}$ $\overline{}$ $\overline{}$ $\overline{}$ $\overline{}$ $\overline{}$ $\overline{}$ $\overline{}$ $\overline{}$ $\overline{}$
1   2   3   4   5   6   7   8   9 10 11 12 13 14 15

16 17 18 19 20 21 22   23 24   25 26 27   28 29 30

?

31 32 33   34 35 36 37 38 39 40   41 42   43 44

.

45 46 47 48 49

WHAT'S THE DIFF?

One of these things is not like the others.
Can you find the imposter?

PLACES, EVERYONE!

Use the word bank and the pictures below to help you fill in the puzzle. Use the order of the pictures as clues. The first one has been done for you.

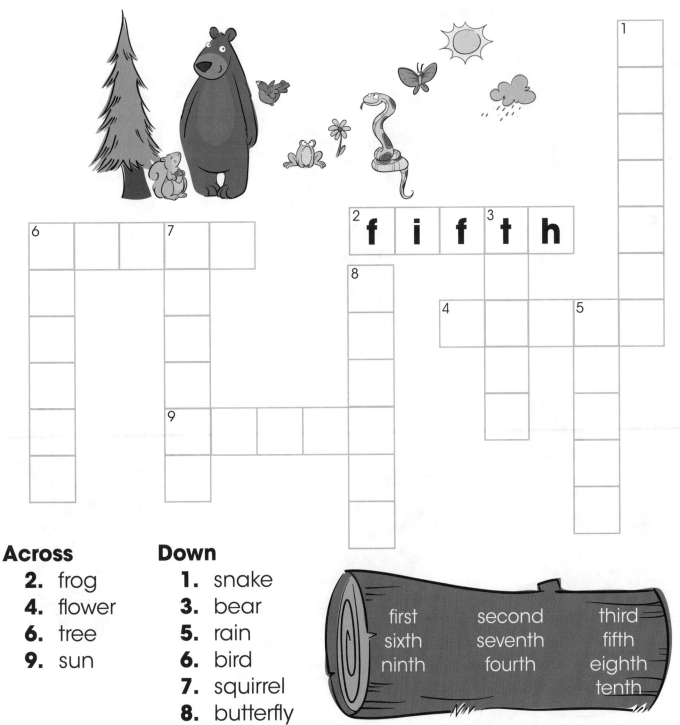

2. **f i f t h**

Across
2. frog
4. flower
6. tree
9. sun

Down
1. snake
3. bear
5. rain
6. bird
7. squirrel
8. butterfly

first   second   third
sixth   seventh   fifth
ninth   fourth   eighth
                      tenth

What's the Diff?

One of these things is not like the others.
Can you find the imposter?

Facing the Sun

Read the clues and use the words in the word box to complete the puzzle.

bee
cheese
eat
sheep
peach
tree
sleep

Across
1. A farm animal.
2. A buzzing bug.
4. A fruit.
6. A very tall plant.

Down
1. At night you _____.
3. A mouse eats _____.
5. You _____ food.

WHAT'S

Can you spot and circle the

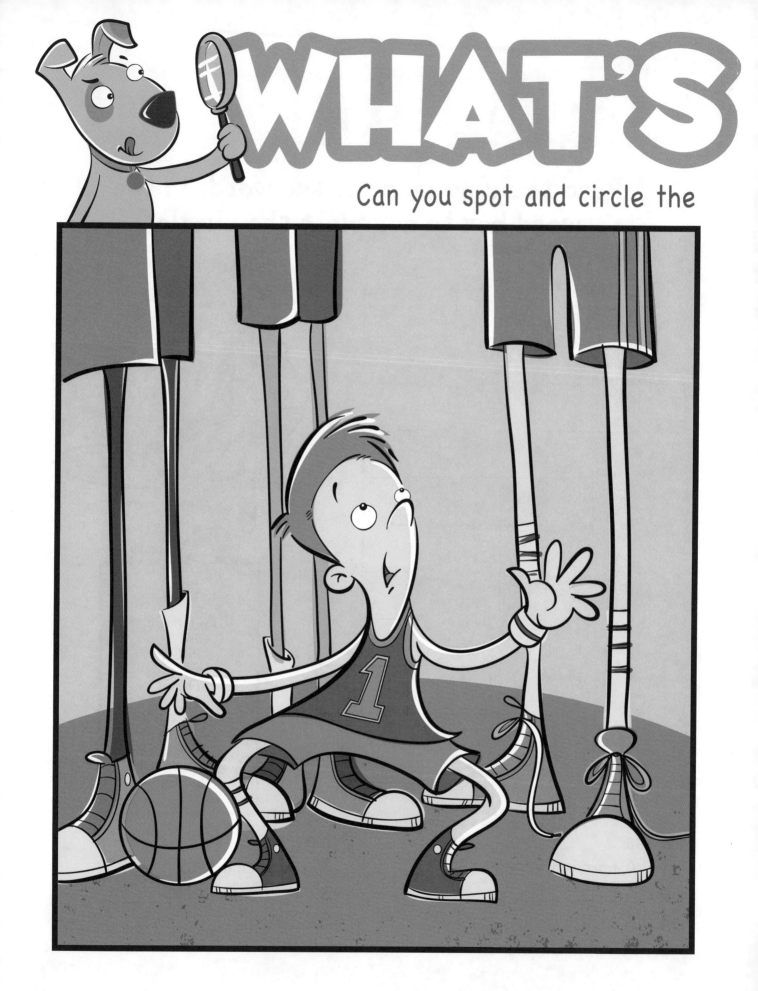

DIFFERENT?

10 differences in these two pictures?

STRETCH!

Read the clues and use the words in the word box to complete the puzzle.

Across

2. A shape that has equal sides.
4. A road.
5. To scatter little pieces.

Down

1. Opposite of **weak.**
2. The sound a mouse makes.
3. A small river.
4. Yell.

STRETCH NOT SQUEEZE!

squeak	square
strong	sprinkle
street	stream
scream	

PRESIDENTS

The names of 5 of America's past presidents have been scrambled below. Each name also has a clue to help you identify the president.

Write each name. Use the word bank.

REGGEO GSWOAHNITN _____
The father of our country

HOJN SMAAD _____
The first president to live in the White House

MABRAAH CNILLON _____
Freed the slaves

KNIRFALN SERVOTLOE _____
Served four times as president

LANROD GRANEA _____
Had been a movie star

Word Bank
Ronald Reagan
John Adams
George Washington
Abraham Lincoln
Franklin Roosevelt

Word Match

Read the two words on each animal. If they have about the same meaning, color the animal brown. If they do not have the same meaning, color the animal red.

chilly
cold

tug
pull

walk
sleep

big
large

dirt
soil

easy
simple

grin
smile

laugh
cry

Cheering Treasure Hunt

Find the **24** hidden items at the game next door.

- ☐ Jalapeño Pepper
- ☐ Peach
- ☐ Baseball Hat
- ☐ Broom
- ☐ Palm Tree
- ☐ Mailbox
- ☐ Party Hat
- ☐ Pushpin
- ☐ Lampshade
- ☐ Pencil
- ☐ Bean
- ☐ Leaf

- ☐ Teepee
- ☐ Slice of Bread
- ☐ Heart
- ☐ Grapes
- ☐ Teacup
- ☐ Rabbit
- ☐ Sock
- ☐ Diamond
- ☐ Carrot
- ☐ Shovel
- ☐ Pennant
- ☐ Butterfly

Birthday Present

Write a word from the word box to complete each sentence.

1. Megan got a new ___ ___ ___ ___.

2. It was a birthday ___ ___ ___ ___.

3. The color is ___ ___ ___ ___.

4. Megan wears a ___ ___ ___ ___ ___ ___ when she rides her bike.

5. She wears elbow ___ ___ ___ ___.

6. She wears ___ ___ ___ ___ pads, too.

Draw a picture of what you want for your birthday.

green

helmet

bike

knee

pads

gift

SECRET WORD

Cross out the letters that spell the name of each item pictured below. Then, use the remaining letters to complete the sentence.

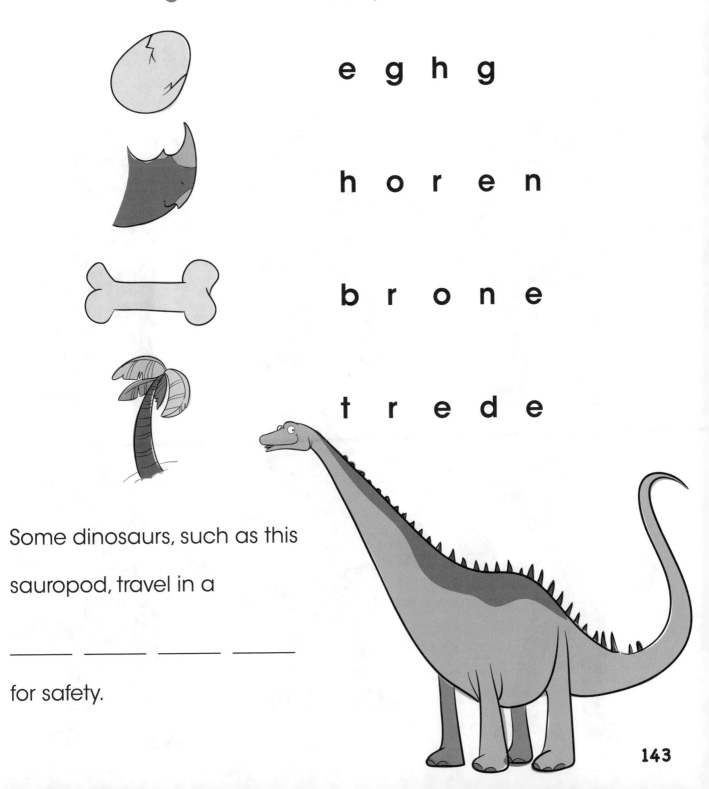

e g h g

h o r e n

b r o n e

t r e d e

Some dinosaurs, such as this

sauropod, travel in a

____ ____ ____ ____

for safety.

WHAT'S THE DIFF?

One of these things is not like the others.
Can you find the imposter?

CAREER TIME

Use the pictures and words in the word box to help you fill in the puzzle.

1.
2.
3.
4.
5.
6.

word box
doctor
teacher
artist
lawyer
singer
chef

1.

2.

3.

4.

5.

6.

WINTER TREASURE HUNT

Find the **28** hidden items on the sledding hill next door.

- Donut
- Mushroom
- Spoon
- Boot
- Popsicle
- Arrow
- Teepee
- Pizza Slice
- Bell
- Lightning Bolt

- Cane
- Banana
- Bowling Pin
- Horse Shoe
- Snail
- Ice Cream Cone
- Macaroni
- Broom
- Pear

- Ring
- Bird House
- Party Hat
- Sailboat
- Flower Pot
- Teacup
- Paintbrush
- Top Hat
- Mitten

Soooo....Cozy

Read the clues and use the words in the word box to complete the puzzle.

bones   stove
boat   home
open   road
hole   notes

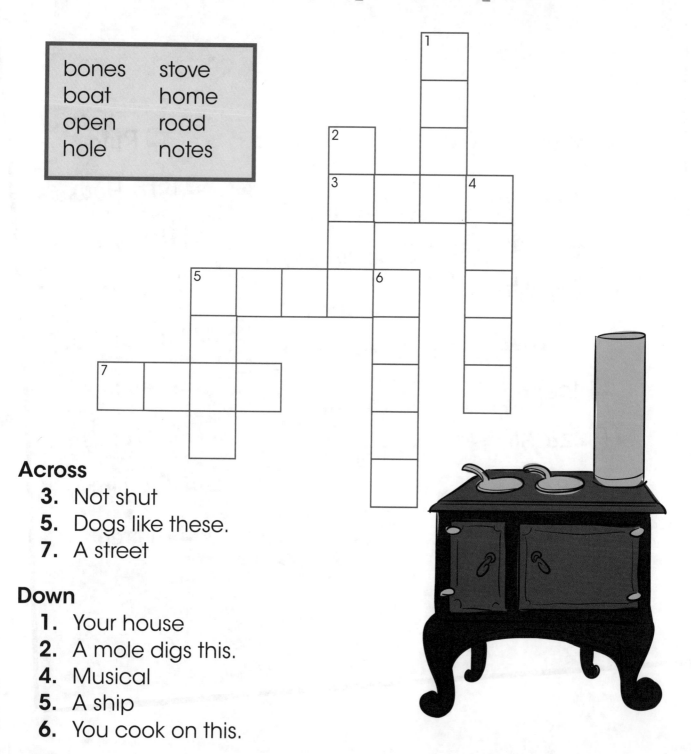

Across
3. Not shut
5. Dogs like these.
7. A street

Down
1. Your house
2. A mole digs this.
4. Musical
5. A ship
6. You cook on this.

MUNCHY ATTACK!

Read the clues and use the words in the word box to complete the puzzle.

| apple | peanut butter | carrots |
| cherry | cheese | banana |

Across

3. It can go in a pie.
5. It is good with jelly.

Down

1. Rabbits like them.
2. It is made from milk.
4. It can be red, yellow, or green.
6. It is yellow and grows in a bunch.

Awesome Accessories

Unscramble the accessories and write them on the lines.

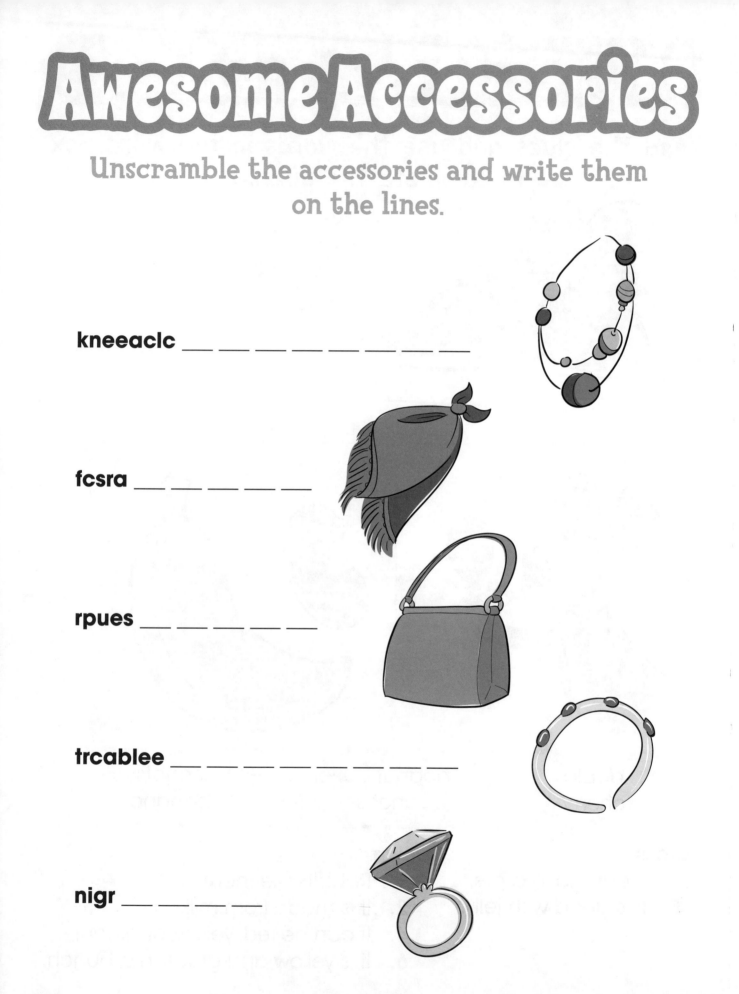

kneeaclc __ __ __ __ __ __ __

fcsra __ __ __ __ __

rpues __ __ __ __ __

trcablee __ __ __ __ __ __ __ __

nigr __ __ __ __

WHEEL OF NOUNS

Try your hand at creating a "wheel of nouns."

1. Begin with the word *cat*.

2. Continue clockwise around the circle by adding a word that is spelled like the previous word except for one letter. Use the picture clues.

3. Make sure that the last word you choose can again turn into the first word with a one-letter change.

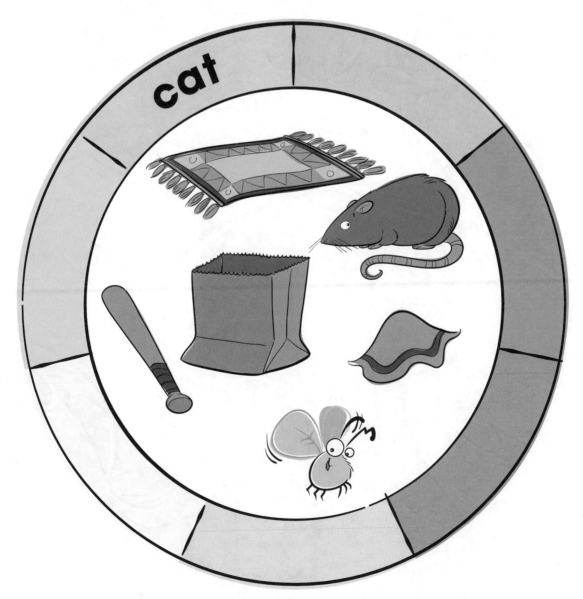

Splashy Treasure Hunt

Find the **25** hidden items in the pool next door.

- ☐ Spoon
- ☐ Mushroom
- ☐ Candy Cane
- ☐ Chicken Leg
- ☐ Mug
- ☐ Sock
- ☐ Fishhook
- ☐ Teacup
- ☐ Mitten
- ☐ Heart
- ☐ Ladybug
- ☐ Lemon Slice
- ☐ Crescent Moon
- ☐ Baseball Bat
- ☐ Paint Can
- ☐ Rabbit
- ☐ Bowl
- ☐ Sun
- ☐ Rainbow
- ☐ Lollipop
- ☐ Leaf
- ☐ Cloud
- ☐ Light Bulb
- ☐ Egg
- ☐ Pine Tree

GOING PLACES

Read the clues and use the words in the word box to complete the puzzle.

airplane
bike
bus
car
truck
boat
balloon

Across
1. It is an automobile.
4. Hot air makes it rise into the sky.
6. This can carry heavy loads on the road.

Down
2. This flies people from city to city.
3. This carries people and big loads on water.
4. It has two wheels and pedals.
5. This takes many people around the city.

Summer Fun

Read the clues and use the words in the word box to complete the puzzle.

Across

2. These buzz around flowers.
3. It is the opposite of **cold**.
4. You might hear them chirp and sing.
6. Bring your lunch outside for this.
7. This kind of day is good for playing outside.

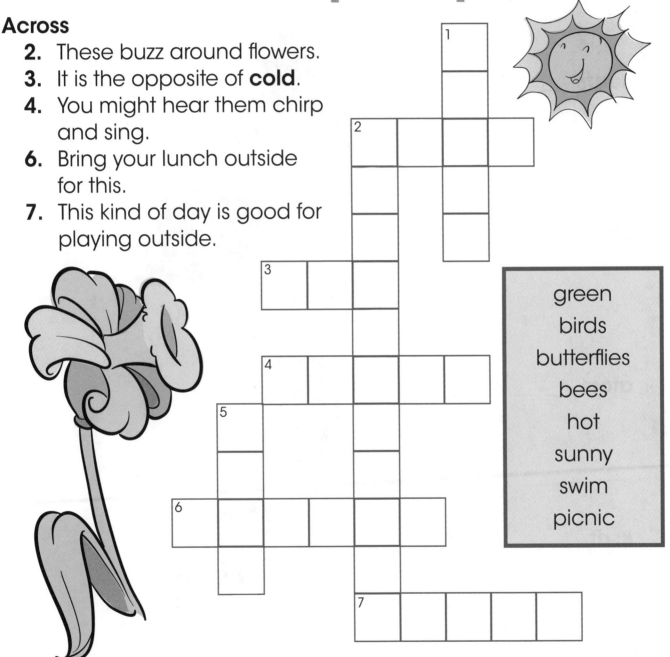

green
birds
butterflies
bees
hot
sunny
swim
picnic

Down

1. Leaves and grass are this color.
2. They flutter their colorful wings.
5. This feels good to do on a hot summer day.

155

Word Scramble

sedrs __ __ __ __ __

oostb __ __ __ __ __

afcrs __ __ __ __ __

ksrit __ __ __ __ __

dbhaedna __ __ __ __ __ __ __ __

156

WORD COMBOS

Each word below can be combined with a word next to it to make a new word. Write some new words.

_____ _____

_____ _____

_____ _____

_____ _____

_____ _____

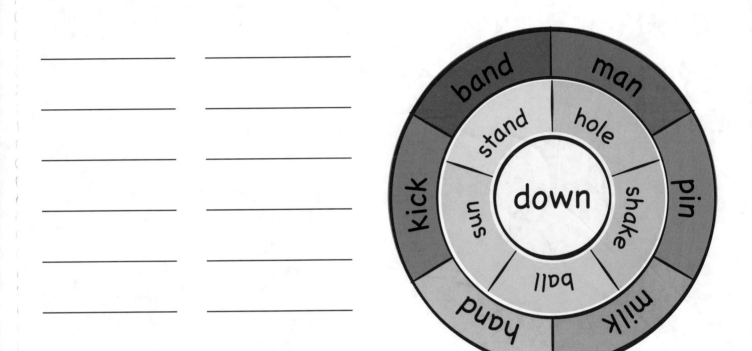

band man stand hole kick down pin sun shake ball milk hand

Draw a picture of one of the words.

dRAGON TREASURE HUNT

Find the **23** hidden items in the scene next door.

- Cherry
- Butterfly
- Paperclip
- Golf Club
- Balloon
- Mitten
- Diamond
- Pizza Slice
- Teacup
- Candy Corn
- Heart
- Megaphone
- Glove
- Stamp
- Sock
- Flower Pot
- Umbrella
- Domino
- Leaf
- Flag
- Sailboat
- Banana
- Party Hat

Art Class

Read the clues and use the words in the word box to complete the puzzle.

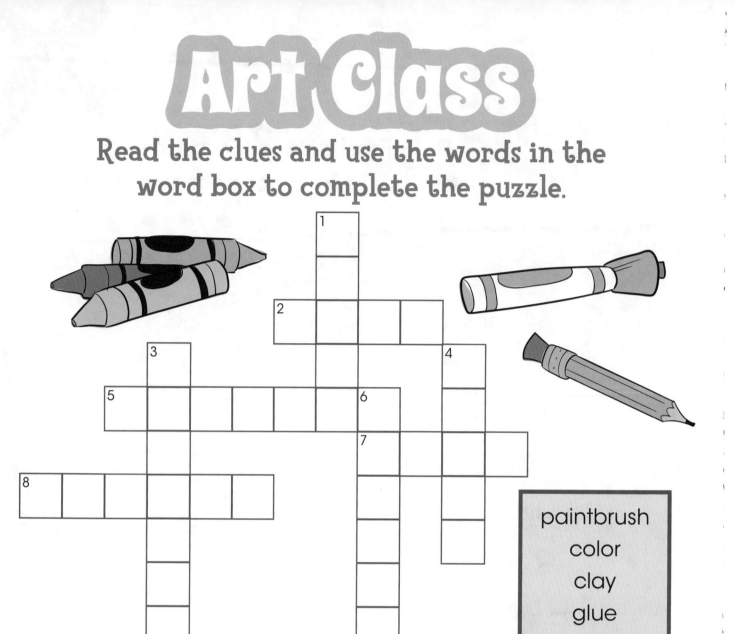

paintbrush
color
clay
glue
paints
chalk
scissors
markers

Across

2. Use this to make paper stick together.
5. Remember to put the caps back on these.
7. Make a pot with this.
8. Use your brushes with these.

Down

1. Purple is one.
3. Use this to spread paint on paper.
4. Make sidewalk drawings with this.
6. Use this to cut scraps for a picture.

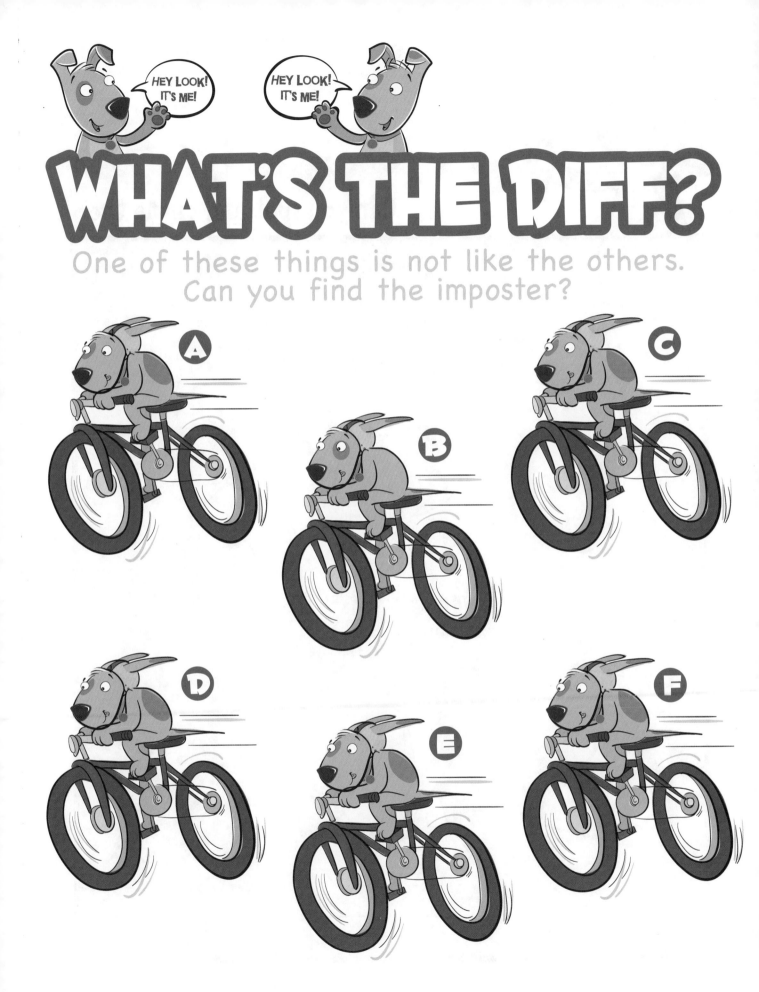

What's

Can you spot and circle the

Different?

11 differences in these two pictures?

HOLIDAYS

Write the holidays from the word box in the puzzle.
Then, find the secret word in the purple box.

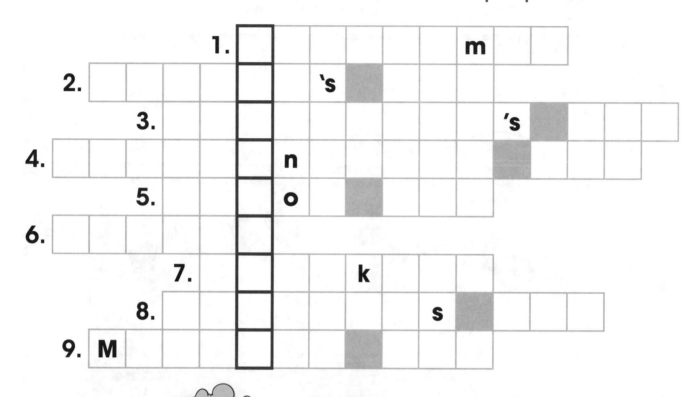

The secret word is _____.

Mother's Day
Father's Day
Veterans Day
Independence Day
Arbor Day
Christmas
Easter
Valentine's Day
Hanukkah

Calendar Clues

Read the clues and use the words in the word box to complete the puzzle.

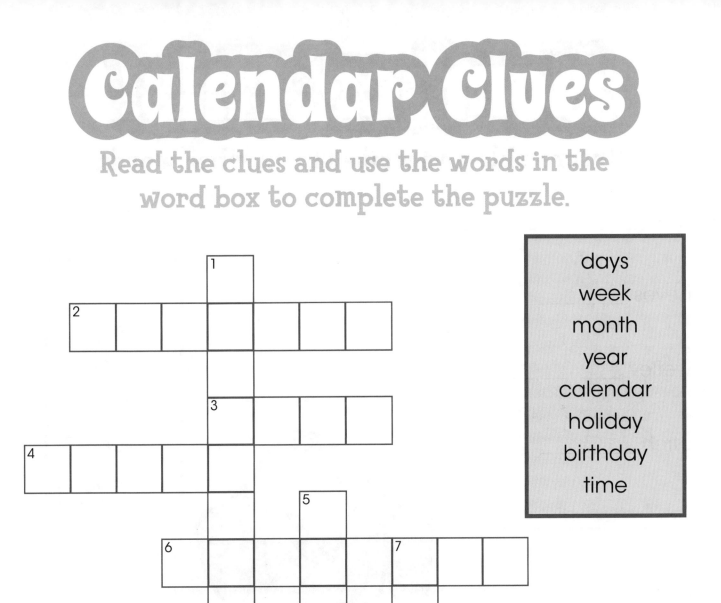

days
week
month
year
calendar
holiday
birthday
time

Across
2. It is a day for celebrating instead of working.
3. It can be measured in days, weeks, months, and years.
4. It can have 28 to 31 days.
6. You can hang it on a wall to keep track of the days.
8. This has twelve months.

Down
1. This is the day you were born.
5. It has seven days.
7. A year has 365 of these.

Number This!

Unscramble and write the number words.

nnei ___ ___ ___ ___

neves ___ ___ ___ ___ ___

wetlev ___ ___ ___ ___ ___ ___

etreh ___ ___ ___ ___ ___

xis ___ ___ ___

etn ___ ___ ___

three

six

seven

nine

ten

twelve

FUNNY FOOD FACTS

Read each sentence. Cross out the noun that doesn't make sense. Find a noun in another sentence that fits but still makes a silly sentence. Write it above the crossed-out word. The first one has been done for you.

1. Lazy people eat ~~chili.~~ **meatloaf**

2. The Easter Bunny's favorite vegetables are chicken.

3. The best fruit to drink is strawberries.

4. If you're scared, don't eat dough.

5. Jellybeans must be a cold food.

6. Dancing cows make blueberries.

7. Cavemen ate meatloaf.

8. Bread is rich because it has watermelon.

9. Milkshakes are an unhappy fruit.

10. Club sandwiches grow on the floor of a barn.

WHAT'S

Can you spot and circle the

DIFFERENT?

10 differences in these two pictures?

BRRR!

Use the word lists to fill out the grid below.
Hint: Count the squares in the grid first to
see where the words will fit.

3-Letters	**4-Letters**	**5-Letters**	**6-Letters**	**7-Letters**
ice	cold	sleet	skated	shivers
ski	melt	spill		
		parka		

170

Love Day

Look at the pictures to complete the puzzle.

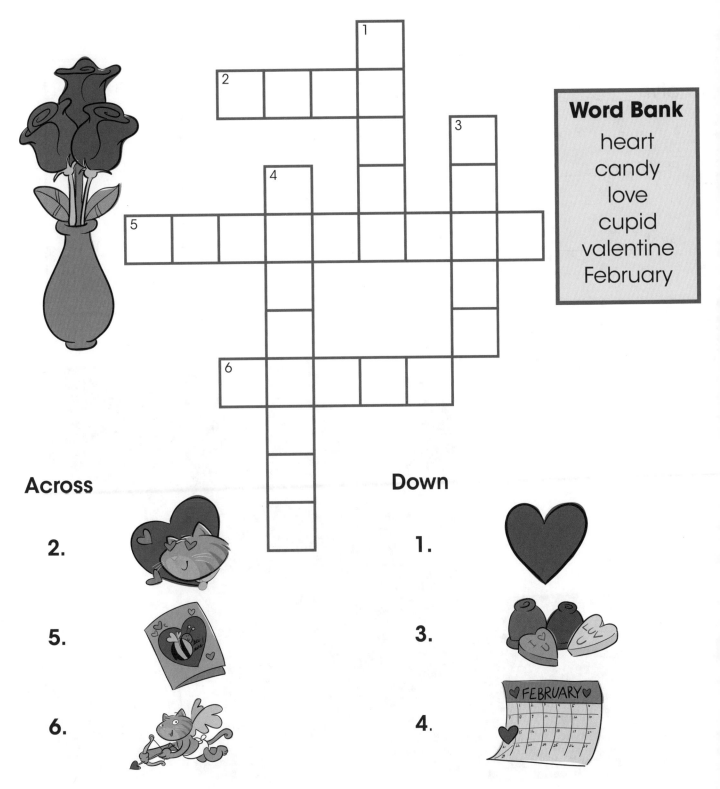

Word Bank

heart
candy
love
cupid
valentine
February

Across

2.

5.

6.

Down

1.

3.

4.

Number This!

Unscramble and write the number words.

neo ___ ___ ___

efvi ___ ___ ___ ___

eeenlv ___ ___ ___ ___ ___ ___

wot ___ ___ ___

theig ___ ___ ___ ___ ___

rufo ___ ___ ___ ___

one
two
four
five
eight
eleven

HOME SWEET HOME

Use the rebuses to discover which nation of Native Americans lived in each kind of home. After you sound out your answer, find the correct spelling in the word bank, and use it to complete each sentence.

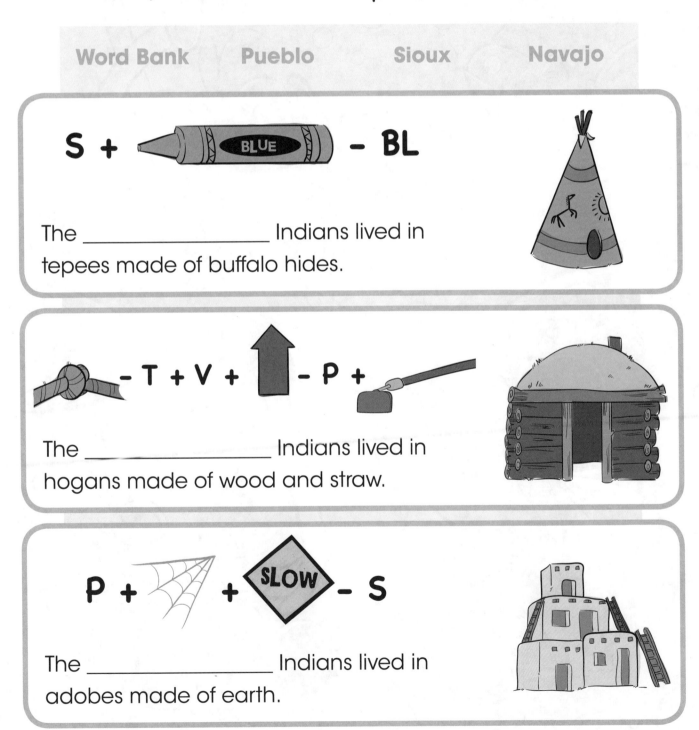

Word Bank　　**Pueblo**　　　**Sioux**　　　**Navajo**

S + [crayon: BLUE] − BL

The _____ Indians lived in tepees made of buffalo hides.

[knot] − T + V + [arrow] − P + [hoe]

The _____ Indians lived in hogans made of wood and straw.

P + [spiderweb] + [diamond: SLOW] − S

The _____ Indians lived in adobes made of earth.

Snorkel Treasure Hunt

Find the **25** hidden items underwater next door.

- ☐ Bowl
- ☐ Banana
- ☐ Heart
- ☐ Snail
- ☐ Sailboat
- ☐ Flower
- ☐ Snowman
- ☐ Cup with Straw
- ☐ Worm
- ☐ Rabbit
- ☐ Christmas Light
- ☐ Pineapple
- ☐ Macaroni
- ☐ Pear
- ☐ Ice Cream Cone
- ☐ Feather
- ☐ Mitten
- ☐ Crescent Moon
- ☐ Cane
- ☐ Pine Tree
- ☐ Fan
- ☐ Pizza
- ☐ Donut
- ☐ Baseball
- ☐ Umbrella

BUSY YEAR

Use the word lists to fill out the grid below.
Hint: Count the squares in the grid first to
see where the words will fit.

4-Letters
year
moon

5-Letters
month
daily
party

7-Letters
holiday

8-Letters
birthday
meetings

Happy Birthday

Look at the pictures to complete the puzzle.

Across

2.

3.

5.

Down

1.

4.

Word Bank

balloons
cupcake
presents
card
party hat

What's the Diff?

One of these things is not like the others.
Can you find the imposter?

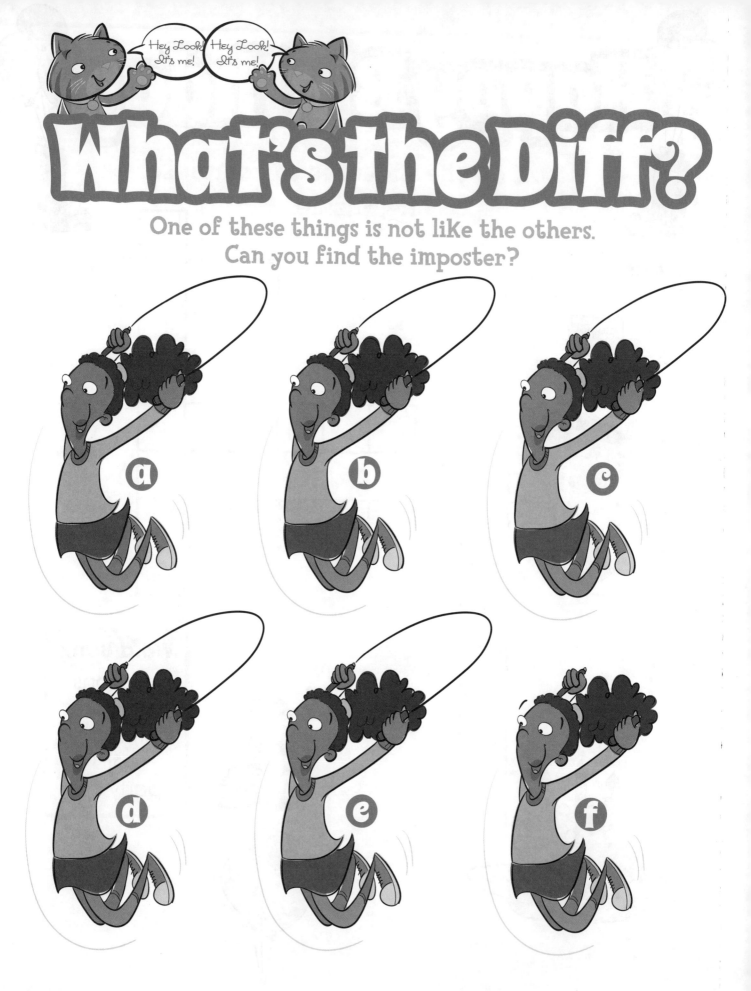

SUMMER FUN

Use the word lists to fill out the grid below.
Hint: Count the squares in the grid first to
see where the words will fit.

3-Letters
hot
tan
run

4-Letters
swim
bike
kite
sail
cone

5-Letters
skate
storm

6-Letters
movies
shorts

icecream

TREE HOUSE TREASURE HUNT

Find the **25** hidden items in the treetop next door.

- ☐ Mitten
- ☐ Leaf
- ☐ Clamshell
- ☐ Ice Cream Cone
- ☐ Envelope
- ☐ Fork
- ☐ Bell
- ☐ Tepee
- ☐ Light Bulb
- ☐ Baseball
- ☐ Fishhook
- ☐ Cup with Straw

- ☐ Mushroom
- ☐ Domino
- ☐ Golf Club
- ☐ Pencil
- ☐ Sock
- ☐ Apple
- ☐ Cherry
- ☐ Top Hat
- ☐ Heart
- ☐ Kite
- ☐ Lollipop
- ☐ Comb
- ☐ Umbrella

AT THE POOL

Use the word lists to fill out the grid below.
Hint: Count the squares in the grid first to
see where the words will fit.

3-Letters	**4-Letters**	**5-Letters**	**6-Letters**	**7-Letters**
tan	pool	slide	lotion	whistle
sun	dive	float		
	raft			
	rest			
	laps			

183

Rainy Day Treasure Hunt

Find the **26** hidden items in the room next door.

- Banana
- Domino
- Toothbrush
- Cheese Wedge
- Pizza Slice
- Sock
- Pine Tree
- Leaf
- Marker
- Mushroom
- Horseshoe
- Smiley Face
- Sail Boat

- Top Hat
- Paint Can
- Comb
- Hockey Stick
- Heart
- Lemon Slice
- Ruler
- Lollipop
- Ring
- Crown
- Soup Can
- Paintbrush
- House

Kaleidoscope of Letters

Each of the pieces of glass in this Kaleidoscope contains a letter. These letters can spell a number of valuable treasures. How many treasures can you form using only letters that are attached to each other by the sides of their triangular shapes? List them on the lines below.

_____ , _____ ,

_____ , _____

Picture Clues

Letters, numbers, and pictures take the place of words in each sentence below. Write each sentence correctly.

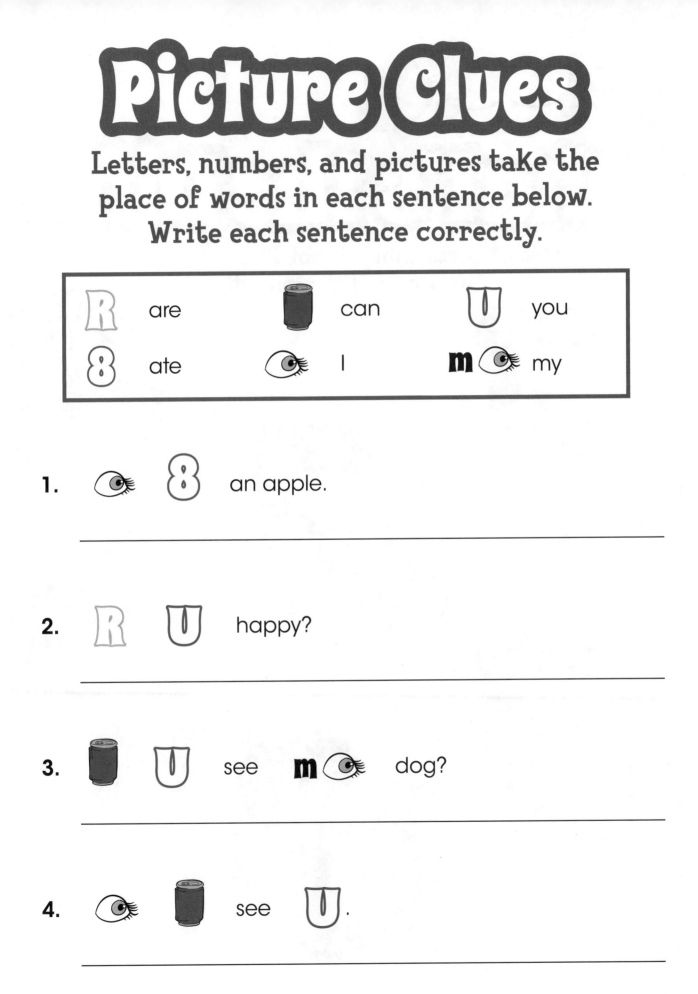

R = are

(can) = can

U = you

8 = ate

(eye) = I

m(eye) = my

1. (eye) 8 an apple.

_____

2. R U happy?

_____

3. (can) U see m(eye) dog?

_____

4. (eye) (can) see U.

_____

Use the words in the box to help you write the name of each picture.

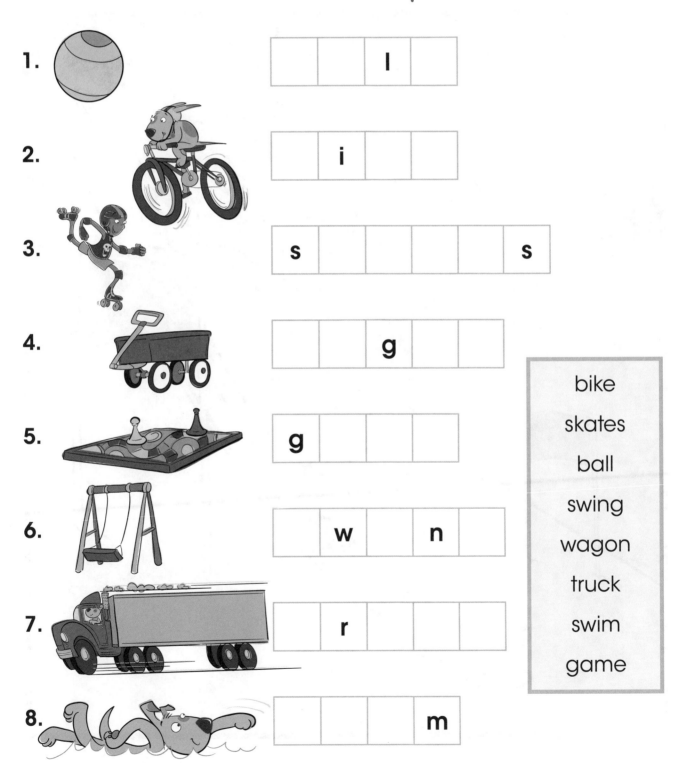

1. | | | l | |

2. | | i | | |

3. | s | | | | | s |

4. | | | g | |

5. | g | | | |

6. | | w | | n | |

7. | | r | | | |

8. | | | m |

bike

skates

ball

swing

wagon

truck

swim

game

What's

Can you spot and circle the

Different?

10 differences in these two pictures?

WILD WEST

Use the word list to fill out the grid below.
Hint: Count the squares in the grid first to
see where the words will fit.

3-Letters	**4-Letters**	**5-Letters**	**6-Letters**	**7-Letters**
map	pipe	range	cowboy	sheriff
aim	spur	sheep	cactus	rawhide
			cattle	
			saloon	

193

CITY ZOO

Use the word lists to fill out the grid below.
Hint: Count the squares in the grid first to
see where the words will fit.

3-Letters	**4-Letters**	**5-Letters**	**6-Letters**	**7-Letters**	**8-Letters**
cub	cage	tiger	snakes	habitat	elephant
pet	deer	teeth	safari	peanuts	

195

Can you spot and circle the

DIFFERENT?

10 differences in these two pictures?

KNOCK, KNOCK!

Knock, knock jokes may be the most classic jokes out there. Try these on your friends for some silly laughs.

Knock, Knock!
Who's there?
Falafel!
Falafel who?
Falafel my bike and cut my knee!

Knock, Knock!
Who's there?
Stopwatch!
Stopwatch who?
Stopwatch you're doing right now!

Knock, Knock!
Who's there?
Ice cream soda!
Ice cream soda who?
Ice cream soda whole world will know what a nut you are!

WHAT WAS THE QUESTION?

Now's your chance to be a comedian! Below are the punch lines to several jokes. But what are the jokes? That's where you come in! Think of the best joke you can that goes with each punch line. Then, tell your jokes to a friend!

_____

"I'm going to pieces!"

_____

A giraffe on roller blades!

_____

A "dive-in" theater.

_____

It laughed hiss-terically.

_____

They get "toad!"

SPACE!

Use the word lists to fill out the grid below.
Hint: Count the squares in the grid first to
see where the words will fit.

4-Letters
Mars
star

5-Letters
Venus
Pluto
Titan
comet

6-Letters
Uranus

7-Letters
Jupiter
Neptune

8-Letters
Milky Way

A S T E R O I D

Equestrian Treasure Hunt

Find the **23** hidden items in the scene next door.

- Pencil
- Mug
- Banana
- Acorn
- Pizza Slice
- Chicken Leg
- Ring
- Screw
- Heart
- Fishhook
- Feather

- Pushpin
- Bell
- Bowl
- Paintbrush
- Candy Corn
- Shovel
- Carrot
- Candle
- Toothbrush
- Mitten
- Pennant
- Sailboat

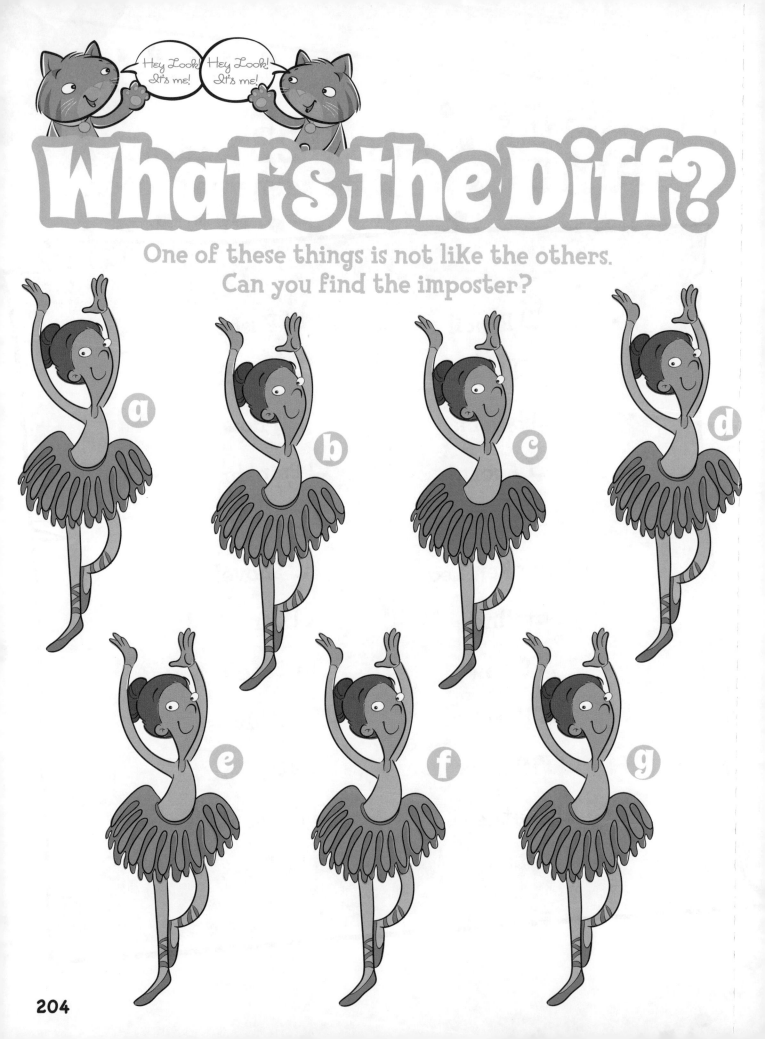

What's the Diff?

One of these things is not like the others.
Can you find the imposter?

204

TOY STORE

Use the word lists to fill out the grid below.
Hint: Count the squares in the grid first to
see where the words will fit.

3-Letters
buy
pay

4-Letters
shop
toys
sell
sale

5-Letters
games
music
guard
clerk
hobby

8-Letters
elevator

SURPRISE!

Use the key to figure out the code and unscramble the answer to the question.

What has two heads, twenty-four legs and sharp, pointy teeth?

KEY	
A	1
B	2
D	3
G	4
H	5
I	6
K	7
N	8
O	9
R	10
S	11
T	12
U	13
W	14
Y	15

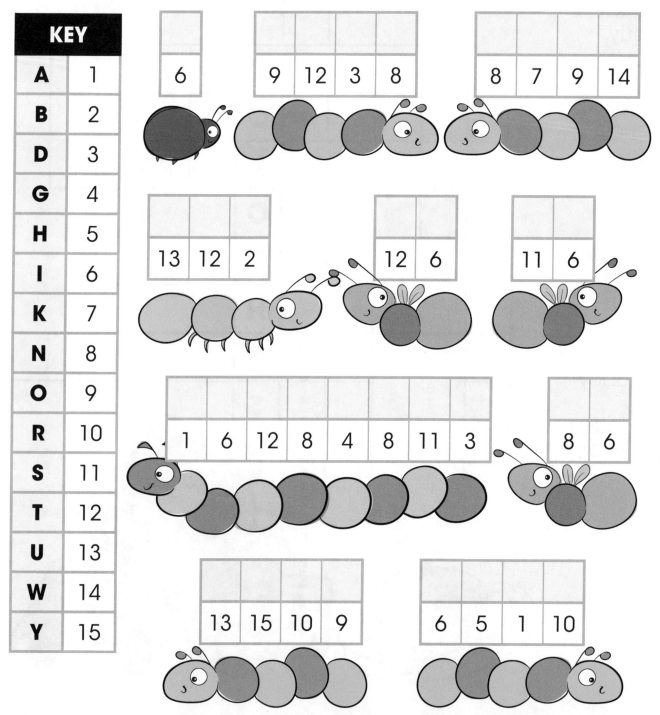

6

9 12 3 8

8 7 9 14

13 12 2

12 6

11 6

1 6 12 8 4 8 11 3

8 6

13 15 10 9

6 5 1 10

CITY GIRL

Read the clues and use the words in the word box to complete the puzzle.

subway
taxi
skyscraper
mall
hospital
bus
museum
zoo

Across
2. This is a place with many stores in one building.
3. This is a place where many animals live.
4. This is a very tall building.
6. Many people ride in this on city streets.
7. People whistle, yell, or wave to get a ride in this thing.

Down
1. This is a place where people go when they are very sick.
2. People visit this place to see very old things.
5. This train goes underground and many people ride on it.

What's

Can you spot and circle the

Different?

10 differences in these two pictures?

209

Bits and Pieces

Write the name of the story on the line.
Choose the names from the word bank.

Cinderella   Three Little Pigs
Wizard of Oz   Hansel and Gretel

L + (- j) + 's =   _____

S + (- b) =   _____

(- ree) + (- n)=   _____

(-) + t + (- b)=   _____

(- pler) + (- ir) + s =   _____

What is your favorite place in the United States?
Draw a picture of it.

ALIEN TREASURE HUNT

Find the **29** hidden items in the school bus next door.

- ☐ Slice of Bread
- ☐ Pushpin
- ☐ Shamrock
- ☐ Teacup
- ☐ Seashell
- ☐ Yard Stick
- ☐ Donut
- ☐ Ring
- ☐ Bowl

- ☐ Top Hat
- ☐ Closed Book
- ☐ Magnifying Glass
- ☐ Paperclip
- ☐ Golf Club
- ☐ Pizza Slice
- ☐ Toothbrush
- ☐ Snowman
- ☐ House
- ☐ Envelope

- ☐ Glass
- ☐ Hockey Stick
- ☐ Pencil
- ☐ Flag
- ☐ Smiley Face
- ☐ Basketball
- ☐ Lollipop
- ☐ Banana
- ☐ Mushroom
- ☐ Heart

RHYME THIS!

Using the pictures as hints, fill in the missing letters of the rhyming words.

	G	U	M

S	N	A	K	E

K	I	T	E

Glamorous Glasses

Add a vowel to each word below to make a new word Gladys can see through her glasses.

Gladys has some goofy glasses. They have springs on them which stretch out words to make room for more vowels.

p_nk   p_rpl_

fr_me   sp_cs

g__k   c_t_y_

DOUBLE DUTY

Homographs are words that have the same spellings but have different meanings and often different pronunciations. Use the clues to find the missing homographs.

Watch the clam ___**close**___ its shell ___**close**___ to the
                                 (shut)   (near)
clownfish.

The prickly porcupine will _____ the _____
                                      (give)   (gift)
to the patient prairie dog.

I _____ the _____ of the whimpering wolf
  (wrapped around)   (cut)
with white gauze.

I will _____ a _____ for providing the polar
        (predict)   (plan)
bear with polka-dotted pajamas.

BARNYARD TREASURE HUNT

Find the **28** hidden items in the barn next door.

- ☐ Light Bulb
- ☐ Heart
- ☐ Sock
- ☐ Slice of Bread
- ☐ Spoon
- ☐ Soup Can
- ☐ Umbrella
- ☐ Mushroom
- ☐ Sailboat

- ☐ Snail
- ☐ Flowerpot
- ☐ Pizza Slice
- ☐ Glove
- ☐ Stamp
- ☐ Toothbrush
- ☐ Envelope
- ☐ Fishhook
- ☐ Crescent Moon
- ☐ Bell

- ☐ Eyeglasses
- ☐ Comb
- ☐ Candle
- ☐ Lollipop
- ☐ Ice Cream Cone
- ☐ Glass with Straw
- ☐ Needle
- ☐ Ruler
- ☐ Pencil

Alike but Different

Write titles for these paintings. The first one has been done for you. Then, draw your own painting and write a title for it.

a hare with hair

_____

_____

_____

_____

_____

_____

_____

_____

Desert Life

Read the clues and use the words in the word box to complete the puzzle.

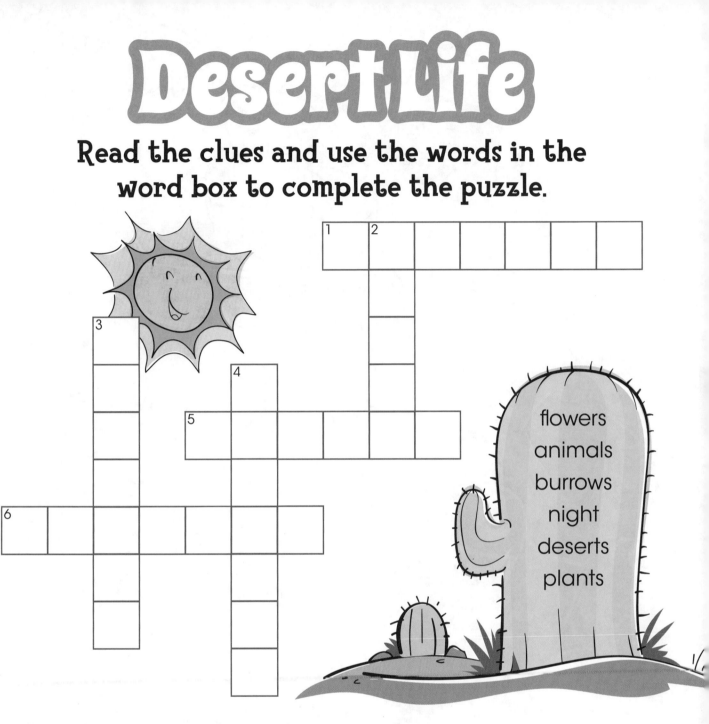

flowers
animals
burrows
night
deserts
plants

Across

1. Desert ____ get water from the food they eat.
5. Desert ____ store water in their leaves, roots, or stems.
6. Many small animals stay in ____ underground during the day.

Down

2. At ____ , the desert animals begin to stir.
3. ____ are very hot and get little rainfall.
4. After it rains, colorful ____ bloom across the desert.

Garden Treasure Hunt

Find the **36** hidden items in the scene next door.

- ❏ Star
- ❏ Toothbrush
- ❏ Butterfly
- ❏ Crayon
- ❏ Pine Tree
- ❏ Comb
- ❏ Stamp
- ❏ Smiley Face
- ❏ Donut
- ❏ Golf Club
- ❏ Book
- ❏ Rabbit

- ❏ Marker
- ❏ Screw
- ❏ Mug
- ❏ Mushroom
- ❏ Spool of Thread
- ❏ Baseball Glove
- ❏ Pizza Slice
- ❏ Worm
- ❏ Clam Shell
- ❏ Carrot
- ❏ Paint Can
- ❏ Bell

- ❏ Glove
- ❏ Hockey Stick
- ❏ Pencil
- ❏ Heart
- ❏ Popsicle
- ❏ Mailbox
- ❏ Cup with Straw
- ❏ Ruler
- ❏ Fishhook
- ❏ Lemon Slice
- ❏ Sailboat
- ❏ Rose

TWIN QUEENS

Circle each letter that makes the sound you hear at the end of  .

The queen has a grin
And a bright golden crown.
But the queen has a twin
Who wears only a frown.

Circle each picture on the crown that ends with the sound of the letter **n**.

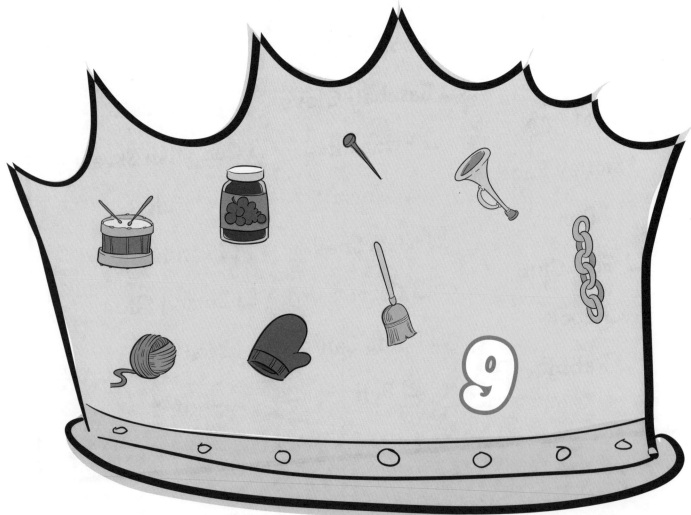

WHO OR WHAT?

Read each riddle below. Use the word bank to identify each creative person or product. Write the answer on the line.

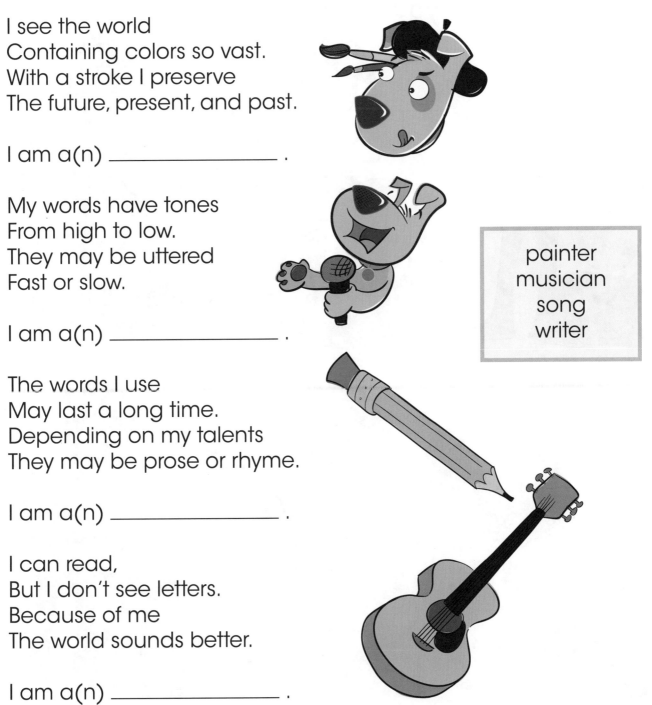

I see the world
Containing colors so vast.
With a stroke I preserve
The future, present, and past.

I am a(n) _____ .

My words have tones
From high to low.
They may be uttered
Fast or slow.

I am a(n) _____ .

painter
musician
song
writer

The words I use
May last a long time.
Depending on my talents
They may be prose or rhyme.

I am a(n) _____ .

I can read,
But I don't see letters.
Because of me
The world sounds better.

I am a(n) _____ .

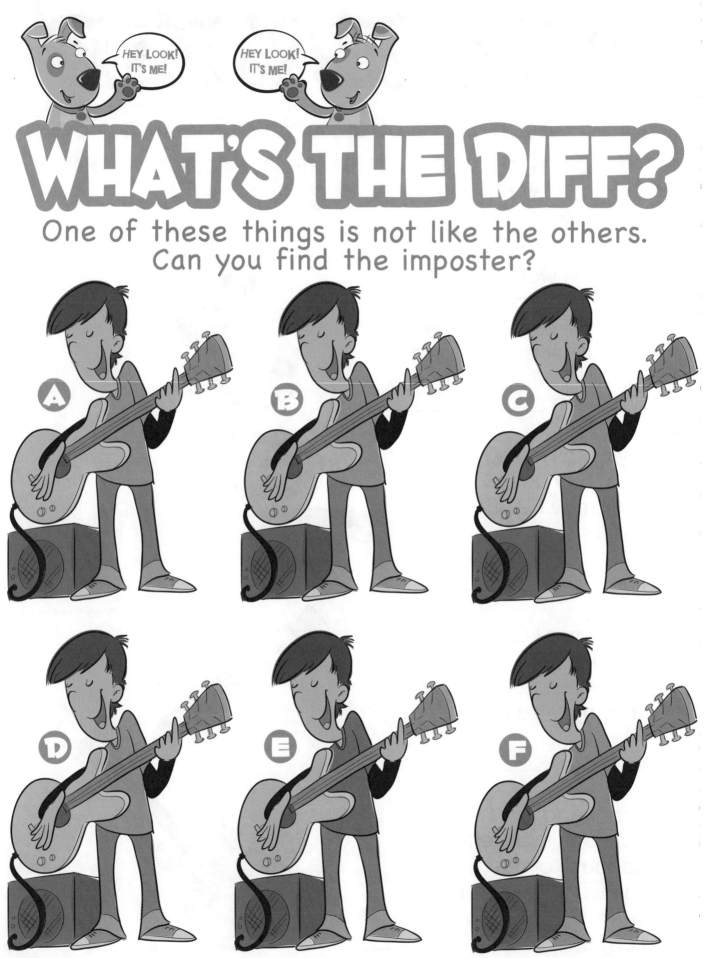

SHARE TWO LETTERS

Each word has two letters in common with the other words. Using the pictures as hints, fill in the rest of the words.

1. `[ ] [ ] [O] [R]`

2. `[ ] [O] [R] [ ]`

3. `[ ] [ ] [O] [R] [ ]`

4. `[ ] [O] [R] [ ] [ ] [ ] [ ]`

5. `[ ] [O] [R] [ ] [ ]`

6. `[ ] [O] [R] [ ]`

7. `[ ] [O] [R] [ ]`

What's

Can you spot and circle the

Different?

12 differences in these two pictures?

ANIMAL ANALOGIES

Use the word bank to help complete these analogies. An analogy is the expression of two like comparisons.

rattlesnake	cow	camel	elephant

A **hill** is to **land** as a **hump** is to a(n) _____.

A **hand fan** is to a **human** as **ears** are to a(n) _____.

Four quarters are to a **dollar** as **four stomachs** are to a(n) _____.

A **chest beat** is to a **gorilla** as a **shaking rattle** is to a(n)_____.

Instrument Chatter

Use the word bank to help solve each riddle about musical instruments.

In my triangle-shaped body
  Many strings have I.
The notes I play
  Are from low to high.

I am a(n)_____ .

High sounds you'll hear
  When you play me.
A long tube with holes
  Is what you'll see.

I am a(n)_____ .

Strum my strings
  And sing in a band.
I play rock and roll
  In a way so grand!

I am a(n)_____ .

You'll hear a bang
  When you hit my top.
Once you hit me,
  It's hard to stop.

I am a(n)_____ .

Deep sounds you'll hear
  When you play me.
Lots of shiny, bright brass
  Is what you'll see.

I am a(n)_____ .

guitar

flute

tuba

harp

drum

RHYME THIS!

Using the pictures as hints, fill in the missing letters of the rhyming words.

F	I	S	H

K	N	E	E

R	O	A	C	H

232

SHARE TWO LETTERS

Each word has two letters in common with the other words. Using the pictures as hints, fill in the rest of the words.

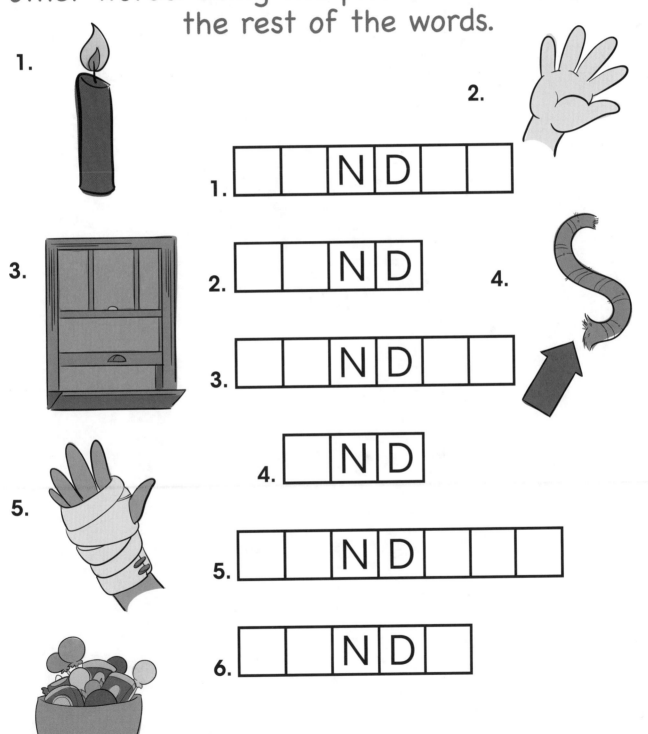

1.

2.

3.

4.

5.

6.

1. ☐ ☐ N D ☐ ☐

2. ☐ ☐ N D

3. ☐ ☐ N D ☐ ☐

4. ☐ N D

5. ☐ ☐ N D ☐ ☐

6. ☐ ☐ N D ☐

SURF'S UP TREASURE HUNT

Find the **24** hidden items in the ocean next door.

- ❑ Mushroom
- ❑ Crown
- ❑ Lollipop
- ❑ Crescent Moon
- ❑ Can of Soup
- ❑ Carrot
- ❑ Heart
- ❑ Bowl with Spoon
- ❑ Bendy Straw
- ❑ Sock
- ❑ Spool of Thread
- ❑ Magnifying Glass

- ❑ Leaf
- ❑ Lemon Slice
- ❑ Pencil
- ❑ Smiley Face
- ❑ Rainbow Cloud
- ❑ Banana
- ❑ Popsicle
- ❑ Feather
- ❑ Pear
- ❑ Paintbrush
- ❑ Horseshoe
- ❑ Glove

Dressing the Part

You want to act in some silly plays. Look at the title of each play below. Write the names of the costumes you would combine to fit the main character of each play.

Below is the inside of a costume closet.

Mouse   **Cowgirl**   **Lion**   **Princess**   **Ghost**   **Dog**

"The Invisible Woman on Her Horse" _____ _____

"The Cat Who Squeaked" _____ _____

"Her Royal Highness Barks up the Wrong Tree"

_____ _____

MYSTERY PICTURE

Read each sentence and cross out the picture.
What picture is left?

1. It is not a toy.

2. It is not foil.

3. It is not boil.

4. It is not coins.

5. It is not soil.

6. It is not oil.

The mystery picture is a _____ .

What's the Diff?

One of these things is not like the others.
Can you find the imposter?

Forest Life

Read the sentences and use the words in the word box to complete the puzzle.

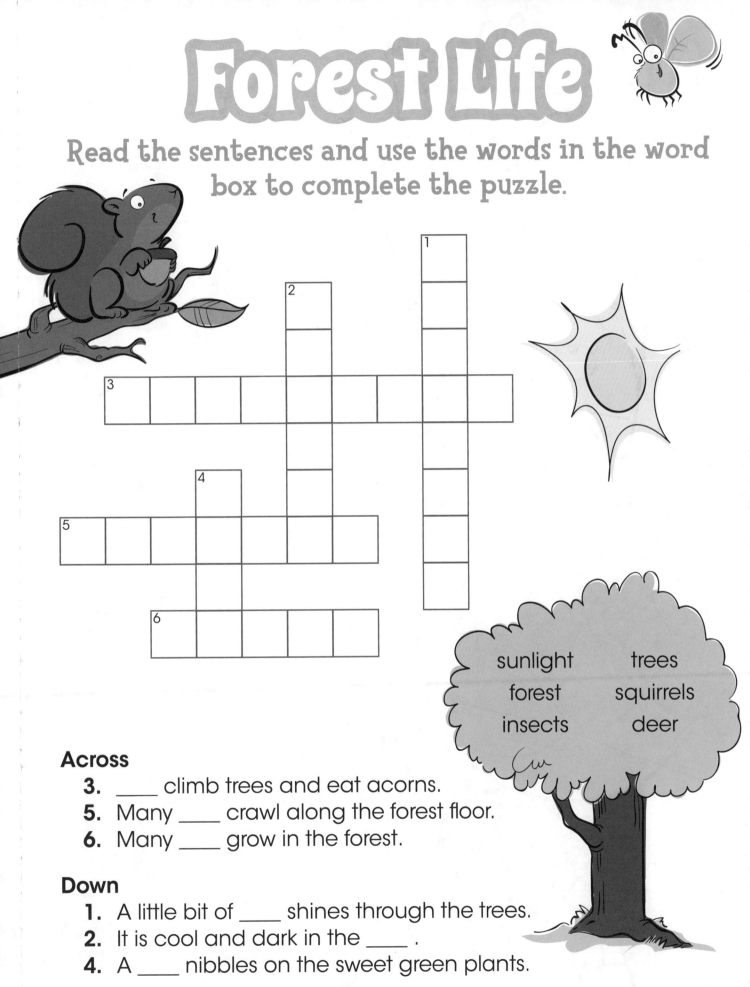

sunlight   trees
forest   squirrels
insects   deer

Across
3. ____ climb trees and eat acorns.
5. Many ____ crawl along the forest floor.
6. Many ____ grow in the forest.

Down
1. A little bit of ____ shines through the trees.
2. It is cool and dark in the ____ .
4. A ____ nibbles on the sweet green plants.

Volleyball Treasure Hunt

Find the **21** hidden items at the game next door.

- ☐ Chicken Leg
- ☐ Domino
- ☐ Open Book
- ☐ Pine Tree
- ☐ Mug
- ☐ Boot
- ☐ Mushroom
- ☐ Heart
- ☐ Banana
- ☐ Balloon

- ☐ Party Hat
- ☐ Flag
- ☐ Lightbulb
- ☐ Lollipop
- ☐ Popsicle
- ☐ Cup with Straw
- ☐ Shovel
- ☐ Kite
- ☐ Ring
- ☐ Sailboat
- ☐ Cherries

RHYME TIME

Using the pictures as hints, fill in the missing letters of the rhyming words.

S	U	N

P	H	O	N	E

C	O	R	N

Nursery Rhymes

Read the clues and use the words in the word box to complete the puzzle.

clock
lamb
hill
sheep
shoe
fiddle
horn
corner

Across

2. Jack and Jill went up the ____.
4. One, two, buckle my ____.
7. Little Jack Horner sat in the ____.

Down

1. Hey diddle, diddle, the cat and the ____.
3. Mary had a little ____.
4. Little Bo-peep has lost her ____.
5. Hickory, dickory, dock, the mouse ran up the ____.
6. Little Boy Blue, come blow your ____.

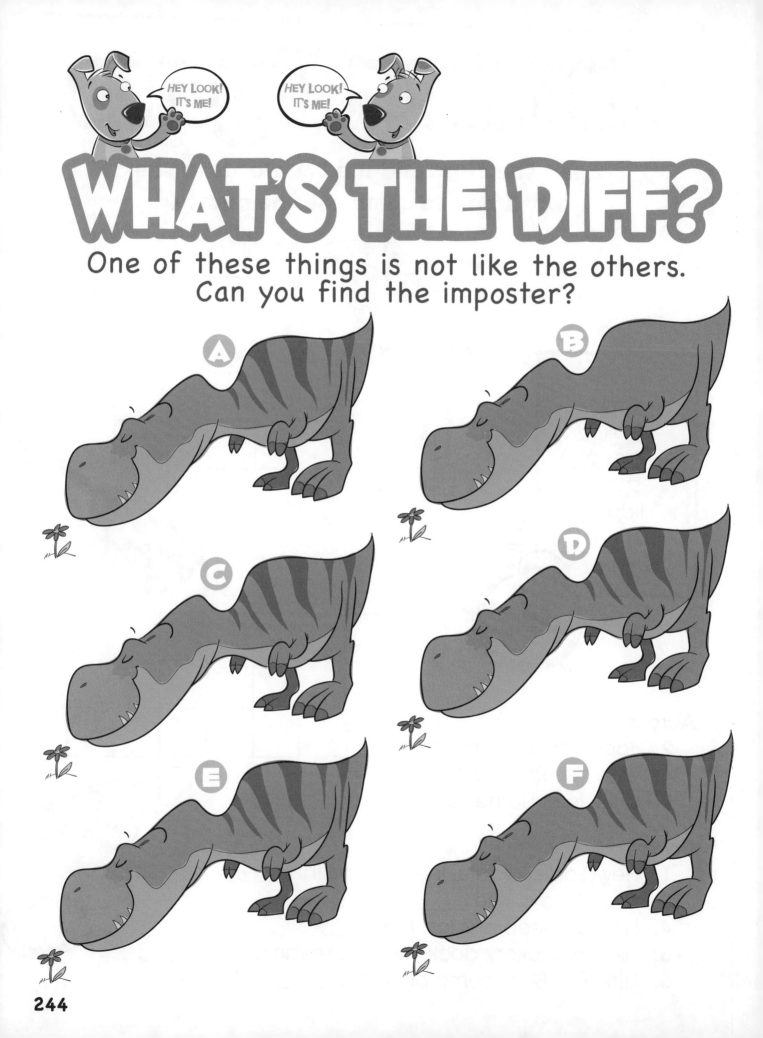

Medieval Fairy Tale

Read the clues and use the words in the word box to complete the puzzle.

castle
king
queen
princess
knights
crown
dungeon

Across

1. I am a male ruler.
2. I am a shiny thing worn on a royal's head.
5. I am the daughter of a queen.
6. I am a house of royalty.

Down

1. We slay dragons and rescue princesses.
3. I am a female ruler.
4. You do not want to be sent here by the king.

246

SHARE TWO LETTERS

Each word has two letters in common with the other words. Using the pictures as hints, fill in the rest of the words.

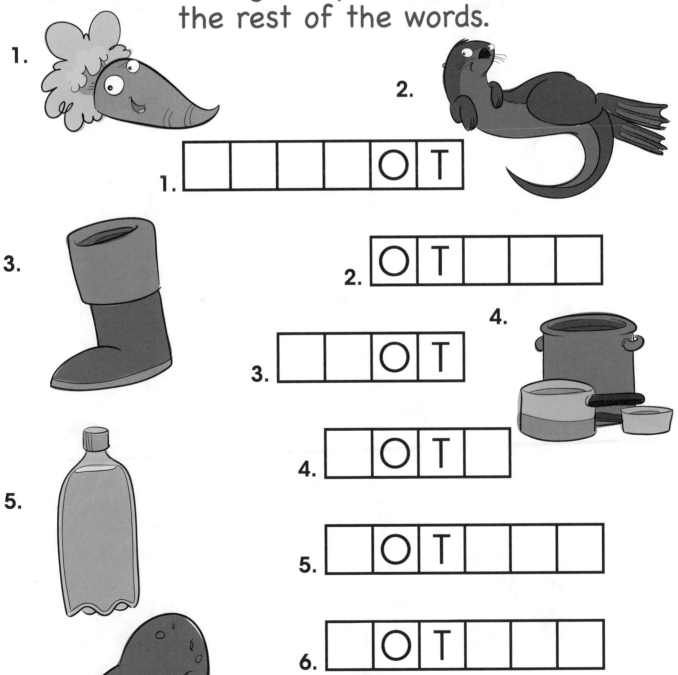

1.

2.

3.

4.

5.

6.

1. ☐ ☐ ☐ ☐ O T

2. O T ☐ ☐ ☐

3. ☐ ☐ O T

4. ☐ O T ☐

5. ☐ O T ☐ ☐

6. ☐ O T ☐ ☐

WHAT'S THE DIFF?

One of these things is not like the others.
Can you find the imposter?

What a Great Place!

Fill in the puzzle with words that name the pictures below. Use the word box to help you.

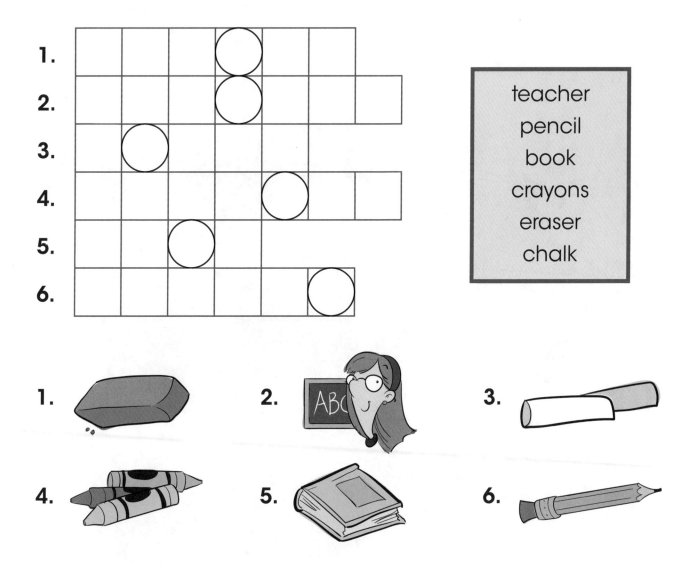

teacher
pencil
book
crayons
eraser
chalk

1.
2.
3.
4.
5.
6.

The letters in the circles going down spell a mystery word. The word names a place where all these things can be found. Write the mystery word.

_____

DIFFERENT?

10 differences in these two pictures?

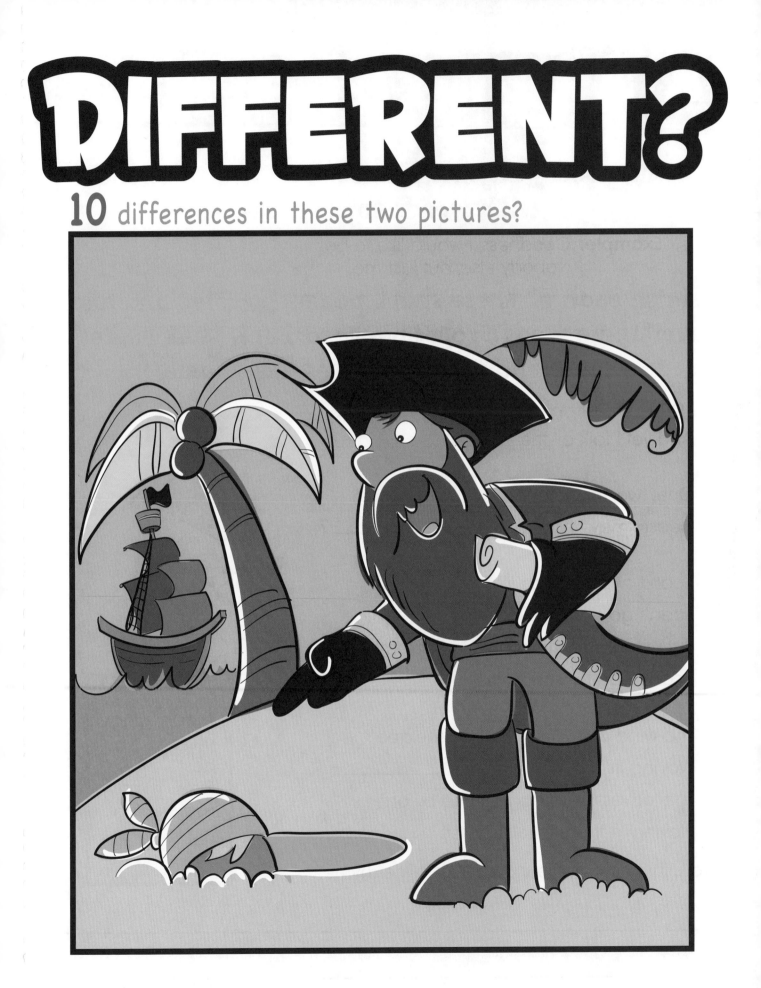

A Rhyme at a Time

Some poetry rhymes. Each set of two lines ends with words that rhyme.

Example: Goodness, I would like to be
Nobody else, but just me.

Finish each of these short poems by selecting and writing a word from the word bank that makes sense and also continues the rhyme.

1. I can't decide what to say,
   And yet I talk all the _____ .

2. One, two, three, four,
   Please, may I have some _____ ?

3. I can't swim outside in the winter;
   I can't go sledding in spring;
   But when autumn comes in September,
   I can hear the school bells_____ .

4. The wind is blowing through the tree,
   Waving its branches for all to_____ .
   The leaves are dragging one by one
   Playing in them in fall can be_____ .

Now, try to create your own 2- or 4-line rhyme.

tee	see
kite	sing
more	day
best	fun
tore	may
nest	ring
me	we
son	run

_____

_____

UNSCRAMBLE!

Unscramble each word.
Be sure it goes with the meaning.

One who plays is called a

lapeyr ___ ___ ___ ___ ___ ___.

A round thing you can kick is a

lalb ___ ___ ___ ___.

prize
winner
player
ball
sailor
candy

A sweet treat to eat is

danyc ___ ___ ___ ___ ___.

Something you can win is a

pzire ___ ___ ___ ___ ___.

A person who wins is the

rnnewi ___ ___ ___ ___ ___ ___.

One who sails a boat is a

ailsor ___ ___ ___ ___ ___ ___.

Summer Fun

Read the clues and use the words in the word box to complete the puzzle.

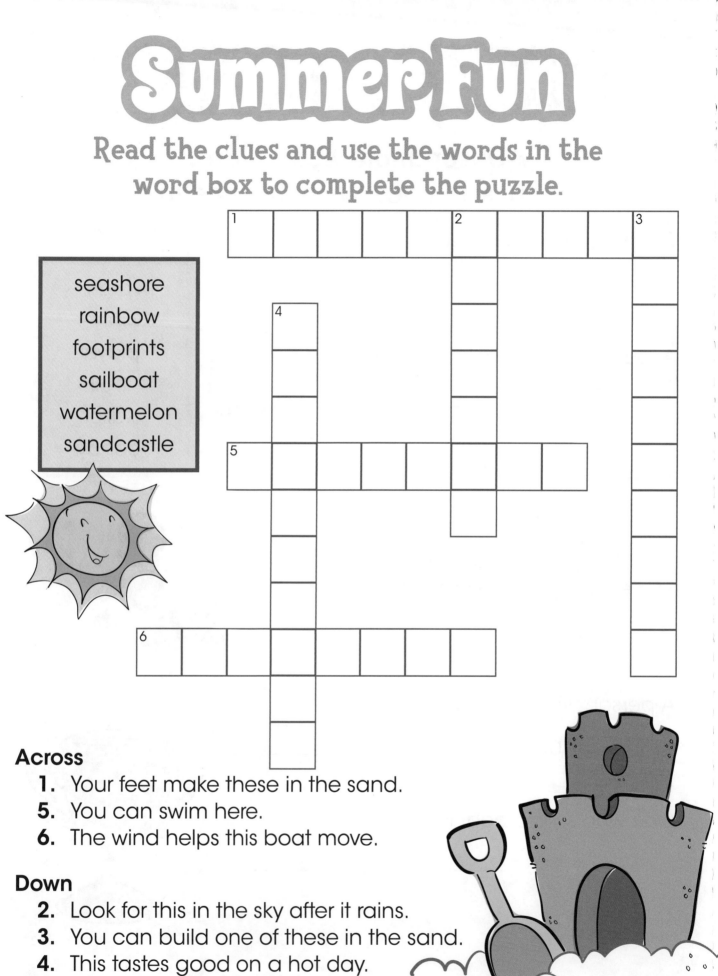

seashore
rainbow
footprints
sailboat
watermelon
sandcastle

Across
1. Your feet make these in the sand.
5. You can swim here.
6. The wind helps this boat move.

Down
2. Look for this in the sky after it rains.
3. You can build one of these in the sand.
4. This tastes good on a hot day.

What's the Diff?

One of these things is not like the others.
Can you find the imposter?

DINO DIG TREASURE HUNT

Find the **25** hidden items in the scene next door.

- ☐ Human Tooth
- ☐ Kite
- ☐ Cane
- ☐ Lemon Slice
- ☐ Piece of Popcorn
- ☐ Smiley Face
- ☐ Key
- ☐ Mushroom
- ☐ Bell
- ☐ Light Bulb
- ☐ Bowl
- ☐ Banana

- ☐ Paintbrush
- ☐ Pear
- ☐ Leaf
- ☐ Tepee
- ☐ Cracked Egg
- ☐ Stocking
- ☐ Button
- ☐ Heart
- ☐ Sailboat
- ☐ Party Hat
- ☐ Soup Can
- ☐ Paperclip
- ☐ Pizza Slice

One Becomes Two

Think of a word that could be the last part of one compound word and the first part of a different compound word. Write the missing word to make two different compound words.

pea _____ cracker

sun _____ pot

cook _____ worm

doll _____ fly

cat _____ bowl

sea _____ fish

bob _____ tail

bird _____ tub

cat	nut	flower	shell
book	fish	bath	house

Think of another compound word and draw a picture for it.

258

GRAND CANYON

Complete each fact about the Grand Canyon by unscrambling the letters at the end of each sentence. Use the word bank if necessary.

Mead	desert	Colorado
Arizona	deep	

The canyon is between 4,000 and 5,000 feet _____ .
(epde)

The Grand Canyon is located in northwestern _____ .
(zanioar)

The canyon was formed by the _____ River. (rodoclao)

The bottom of the Grand Canyon is mostly _____ .
(seetrd)

The lake that forms at the southern end of the Grand Canyon is

called Lake _____ . (deam)

What kind of animals do you think live in the Grand Canyon?
Draw a picture of one.

What's the Diff?

One of these things is not like the others.
Can you find the imposter?

LAND AND WATER

Read the clues and use the words in the word box to complete the puzzle.

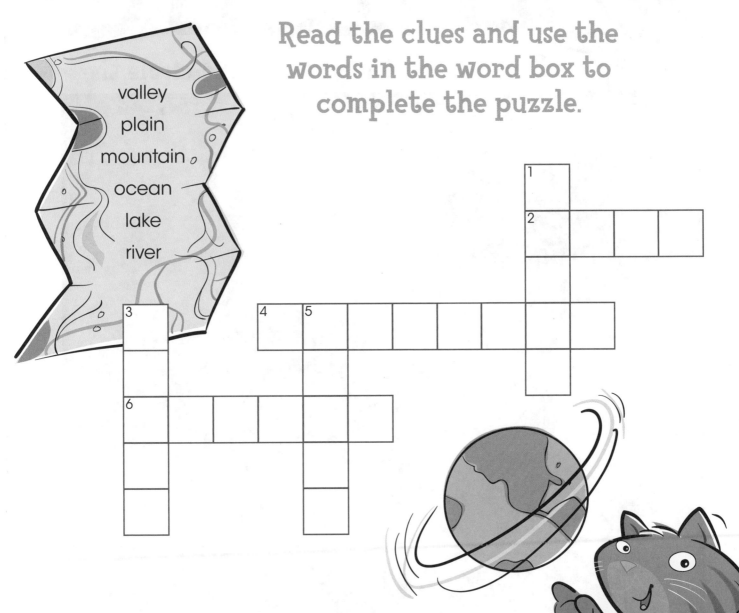

valley
plain
mountain
ocean
lake
river

Across

  2. This is a body of fresh water surrounded by land.
  4. This is a very high hill.
  6. This is low land between mountains or hills.

Down

  1. This is a very flat stretch of land.
  3. This is a flowing stream of water.
  5. This is a large body of salt water.

What's

Can you spot and circle the

Different?

10 differences in these two pictures?

Musical Instruments

Use the code to find out which instruments the children play.

Eric plays the ___ ___ ___ ___ ___.
          11   6   1   9 10

Susan plays the ___ ___ ___ ___ ___ ___.
               5 15   6 14   1 12

Allison prefers the ___ ___ ___ ___ ___ ___.
                   16   6 10   7   6   9

Greg plays the ___ ___ ___ ___ ___.
              3 12 15   8 13

Sumi has a ___ ___ ___ ___ ___.
           2   4   7   7 10

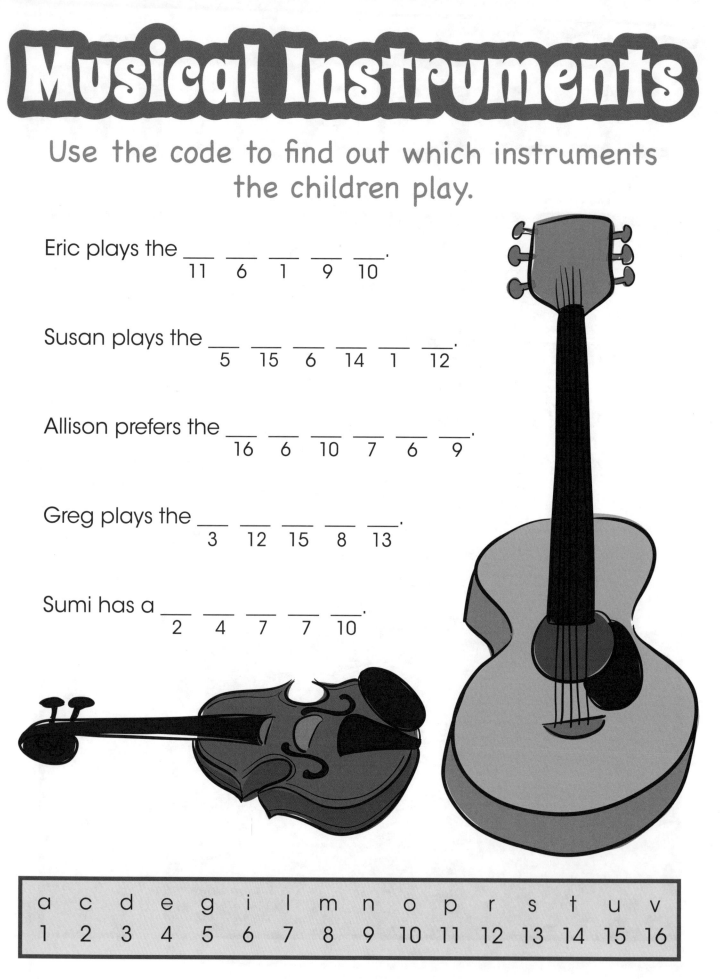

a	c	d	e	g	i	l	m	n	o	p	r	s	t	u	v
1	2	3	4	5	6	7	8	9	10	11	12	13	14	15	16

Musical Instruments

Use the code to find out which instruments the children play.

Scotty plays a $\underline{\quad}_{14}$ $\underline{\quad}_{12}$ $\underline{\quad}_{15}$ $\underline{\quad}_{8}$ $\underline{\quad}_{11}$ $\underline{\quad}_{4}$ $\underline{\quad}_{14}$.

Kelsey has an $\underline{\quad}_{1}$ $\underline{\quad}_{2}$ $\underline{\quad}_{2}$ $\underline{\quad}_{10}$ $\underline{\quad}_{12}$ $\underline{\quad}_{3}$ $\underline{\quad}_{6}$ $\underline{\quad}_{10}$ $\underline{\quad}_{9}$.

Nick is learning to play the $\underline{\quad}_{10}$ $\underline{\quad}_{12}$ $\underline{\quad}_{5}$ $\underline{\quad}_{1}$ $\underline{\quad}_{9}$.

Howard plays the $\underline{\quad}_{14}$ $\underline{\quad}_{12}$ $\underline{\quad}_{6}$ $\underline{\quad}_{1}$ $\underline{\quad}_{9}$ $\underline{\quad}_{5}$ $\underline{\quad}_{7}$ $\underline{\quad}_{4}$.

Annie likes to play the $\underline{\quad}_{5}$ $\underline{\quad}_{10}$ $\underline{\quad}_{9}$ $\underline{\quad}_{5}$.

a	c	d	e	g	i	l	m	n	o	p	r	s	t	u	v
1	2	3	4	5	6	7	8	9	10	11	12	13	14	15	16

HALLOWEEN FUN

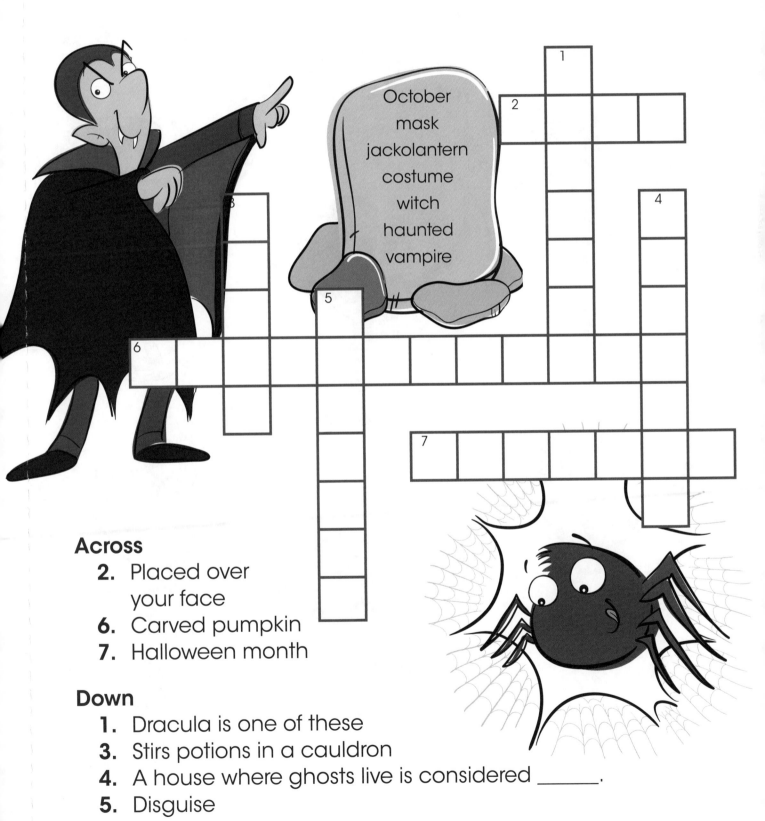

October
mask
jackolantern
costume
witch
haunted
vampire

Across
2. Placed over your face
6. Carved pumpkin
7. Halloween month

Down
1. Dracula is one of these
3. Stirs potions in a cauldron
4. A house where ghosts live is considered _____.
5. Disguise

FOUR SQUARE

Starting with the top word in each square, change one letter at a time until the top word becomes the bottom word.

B	O	N	E
C	A	P	S

T	A	L	K
D	I	M	E

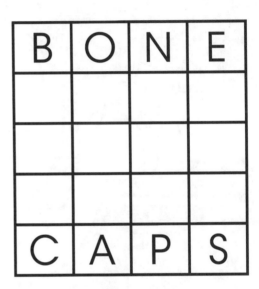

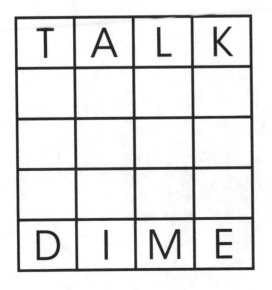

Musical Treasure Hunt

Find the **29** hidden items in the classroom next door.

- ☐ Teacup
- ☐ Flower Pot
- ☐ Sailboat
- ☐ Pencil
- ☐ Book
- ☐ Lollipop
- ☐ Screw
- ☐ Lemon Wedge
- ☐ Pizza Slice
- ☐ Feather
- ☐ Crayon

- ☐ Hockey Stick
- ☐ Starfish
- ☐ Music Note
- ☐ Butterfly
- ☐ Leaf
- ☐ Cherry
- ☐ Popsicle
- ☐ Paintbrush

- ☐ Snake
- ☐ Snowman
- ☐ Umbrella
- ☐ Donut
- ☐ Mushroom
- ☐ Candle
- ☐ Golf Club
- ☐ Stocking
- ☐ Flashlight
- ☐ Baseball Hat

LETTER CHANGE

Starting with the top word in each square, change one letter at a time until the top word becomes the bottom word.

R	I	P	E
P	A	L	M

M	I	C	E
L	A	R	K

What's the Diff?

One of these things is not like the others.
Can you find the imposter?

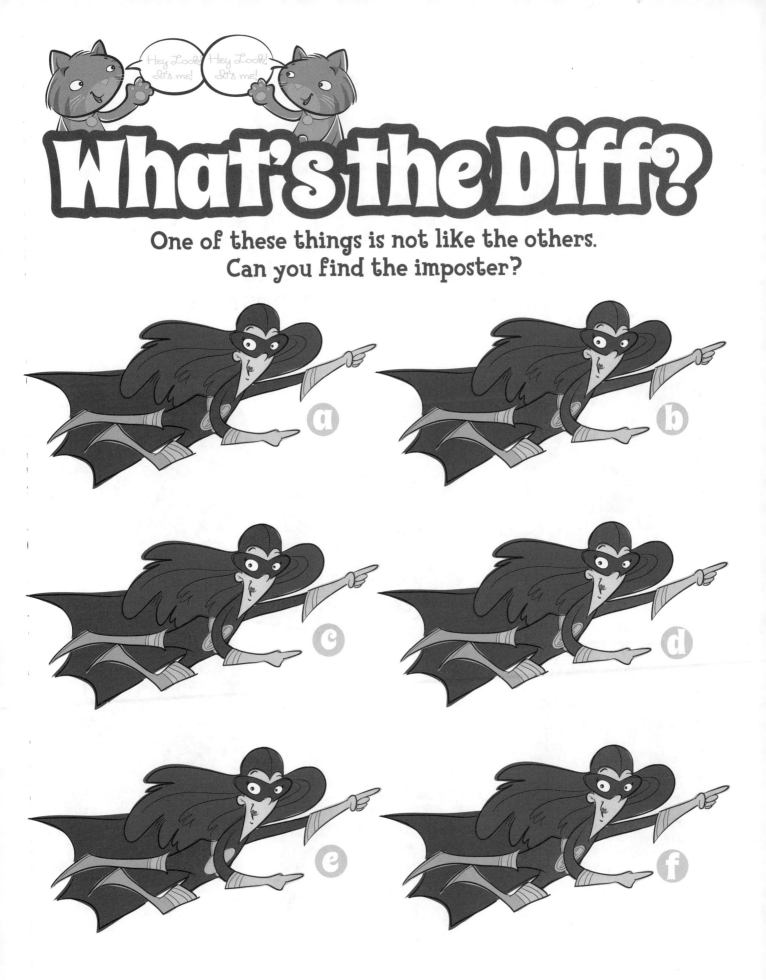

PUZZLE CLUES

Use the pictures as clues to fill in the crossword puzzle.

1 ACROSS

2 ACROSS

1 DOWN

3 DOWN

4 DOWN

5 DOWN

6 ACROSS

7 ACROSS

FALL FUN TREASURE HUNT

Find the **23** hidden items in the leaf pile next door.

- Balloon
- Teacup
- Popsicle
- Pencil
- Paperclip
- Mitten
- Flowerpot
- Comb
- Marker
- Eyeglasses
- Bowl
- Heart
- Worm
- Bell
- Mushroom
- Toothbrush
- Light bulb
- Pine Tree
- Banana
- Crescent Moon
- Basketball
- Carrot
- Whistle

JUMBLED DANGERS

Each set of jumbled letters below represents two possible dangers to explorers. Use the clue to help you unscramble the letters to name the two dangers. Use all the letters, but use each letter only once.

Clue: Both are cats, but one is "king."
PLEIALRONDO

_____ _____

Clue: Both are man-eating and live in or near water.
PIROOEIACCRNDALH

_____ _____

Clue: Both can make you "shake, rattle, and roll."
OEVLCTAUAHEORANQK

_____ _____

Clue: Both like to "monkey around."
BLOBAOIOGRLAN

_____ _____

What is a place you would like to explore?
Draw a picture of this place.

Keys to Spelling

Use the numbers on the Keys to spell out some words about music.

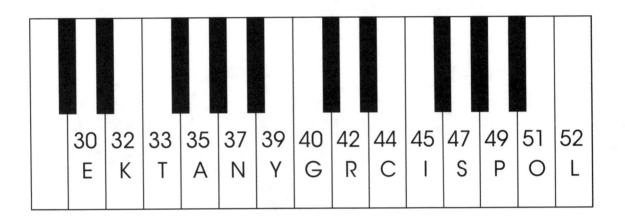

47 51 37 40 __ __ __ __

32 30 39 47 __ __ __ __

49 45 35 37 51 __ __ __ __ __

42 30 44 45 33 35 52 __ __ __ __ __ __ __

What is your favorite type of musical instrument? Draw a picture.

WHAT'S THE DIFF?

One of these things is not like the others.
Can you find the imposter?

Mystery Word

Write the beginning letter of each word in the boxes to make a new word.

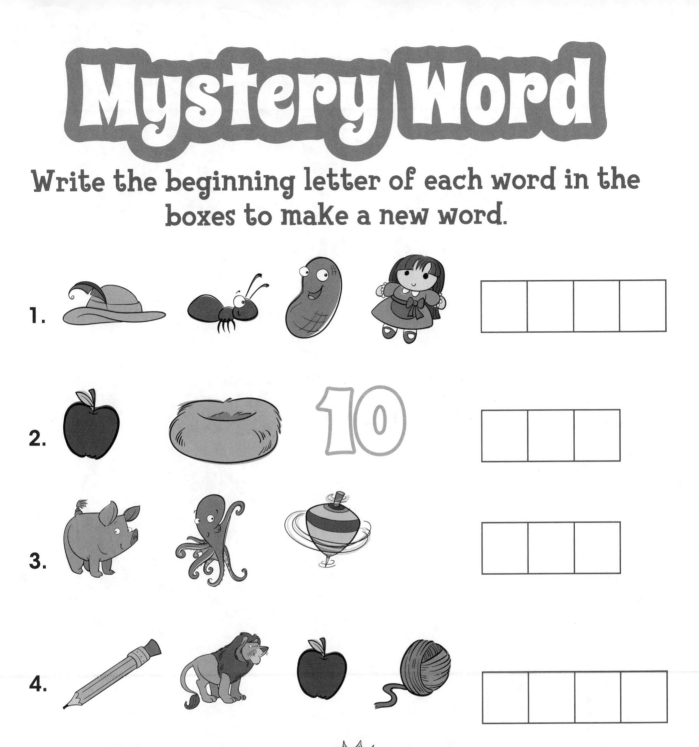

1.

2.

3.

4.

5.

Write the first letter of each word you wrote to find the

mystery word. ___ ___ ___ ___ ___.

Thrill Ride Treasure Hunt

Find the **26** hidden items on the roller coaster next door.

- ☐ Whistle
- ☐ Mushroom
- ☐ Stamp
- ☐ Soup Can
- ☐ Pizza Slice
- ☐ Heart
- ☐ Lightbulb
- ☐ Ring
- ☐ Hammer
- ☐ Envelope
- ☐ Rolling Pin
- ☐ Pennant
- ☐ Snail

- ☐ Fishhook
- ☐ Sock
- ☐ Book
- ☐ Donut
- ☐ Crescent Moon
- ☐ Flag
- ☐ Ruler
- ☐ Paperclip
- ☐ Crown
- ☐ Toothbrush
- ☐ Mailbox
- ☐ Popsicle
- ☐ Teacup

CHANGE A LETTER

Starting with the top word in each square, change one letter at a time until the top word becomes the bottom word.

L	I	S	T
M	A	N	E

T	I	M	E
F	E	L	L

SPACE LINGO

Carefully follow each direction on this and the next page to form words that are important for successful space travel.

1. Write a 3-letter word that means "a rule we must obey." __ __ __

   Add the name of the meal you eat at noon. __ __ __ __ __

   Remove two letters to form a word that marks the beginning

   of a space trip. __ __ __ __ __ __

2. Write a 4-letter word that refers to a bottle stopper. __ __ __ __

   Jumble those letters to form a word that means "a stone." __ __ __ __

   Add "et" for the power source for a spaceship. __ __ __ __ __ __

3. Write a 5-letter verb that shows how you might cook turkey or chicken.

   __ __ __ __ __

   Add a fish often used in sandwiches. __ __ __ __

   Jumble the letters and you will have the name of a space crew member.

   __ __ __ __ __ __ __ __ __

"LINGO" MEANS "SPEECH"

4. Write a verb that means "to sulk." ___ ___ ___ ___

   Change two letters to form a word that means "to close." ___ ___ ___ ___

   Add a word that means "to allow." ___ ___ ___

   Jumble three letters to name an important space vehicle.

   ___ ___ ___ ___ ___ ___ ___

5. Write a word that names the punctuation used to separate words in a list. ___ ___ ___ ___ ___

   Add a word that means the opposite of "over."

   ___ ___ ___ ___ ___

   Remove a letter to show the leader of a space crew.

   ___ ___ ___ ___ ___ ___ ___ ___ ___

Where in space would you like to travel? Draw a picture of what you might explore.

WHAT'S

Can you spot and circle the

DIFFERENT?

10 differences in these two pictures?

GHOST JOKE

Use the secret code to reveal the answer to the spooky joke. Then, tell the joke to your friends around the campfire!

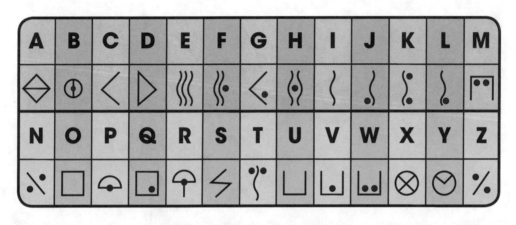

What happens when a ghost
gets lost in a fog?

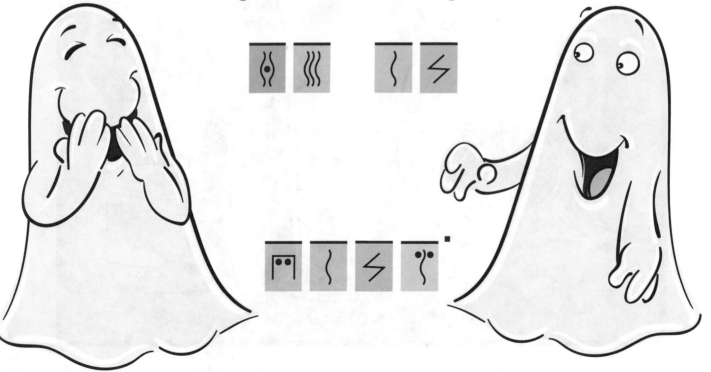

CRACK THE CODE

Solve the secret code below to unlock the answer to a funny joke.

Why did the cookie go to the hospital?

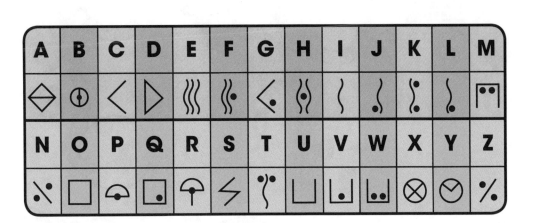

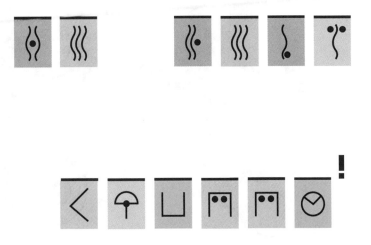

HE FELT CRUMMY!

292

PICTURE CLUES

Use the pictures as clues to fill in the crossword puzzle.

1 ACROSS

2 ACROSS

1 DOWN

3 DOWN

4 DOWN

5 DOWN

6 ACROSS

7 ACROSS

Victory Treasure Hunt

Find the **25** hidden items on the bus next door.

- ☐ Party Hat
- ☐ Stamp
- ☐ Baseball
- ☐ Butterfly
- ☐ Music Note
- ☐ Football
- ☐ Sailboat
- ☐ Shell
- ☐ Palm Tree
- ☐ Magnifying Glass
- ☐ Banana
- ☐ Teacup

- ☐ Envelope
- ☐ Grapes
- ☐ Crescent Moon
- ☐ Ruler
- ☐ Hot Pepper
- ☐ Feather
- ☐ Hockey Stick
- ☐ Rabbit
- ☐ Pencil
- ☐ Donut
- ☐ Candy Cane
- ☐ Mop
- ☐ Marker

SHARE TWO LETTERS

Each word has two letters in common with the other words. Using the pictures as hints, fill in the rest of the words.

1.

1. ☐ A S ☐ ☐

2. ☐ A S ☐

3. ☐ A S ☐

4. ☐ ☐ A S ☐

5. ☐ A S ☐ ☐ ☐ ☐

6. ☐ ☐ A S ☐

7. ☐ A S ☐

GOALIE TREASURE HUNT

Find the **21** hidden items at the soccer field next door.

- ☐ Open Book
- ☐ House
- ☐ Baseball Cap
- ☐ Crayon
- ☐ Flowerpot
- ☐ Flag
- ☐ Ice Cream Cone
- ☐ Arrow
- ☐ Cotton Candy
- ☐ Bendy Straw
- ☐ Heart
- ☐ Comb
- ☐ Fishhook
- ☐ Cherry
- ☐ Paperclip
- ☐ Suspension Bridge
- ☐ Whistle
- ☐ Hockey Stick
- ☐ Domino
- ☐ Pencil
- ☐ Sailboat

LETTER CHANGE

Starting with the top word in each square, change one letter at a time until the top word becomes the bottom word.

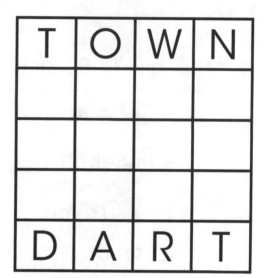

T	O	W	N
D	A	R	T

F	A	R	M
T	I	M	E

Fun Foods

Write each word in the correct place.

| popcorn | ice cream | lollipop |
| candy | cookie | cake |

Cute Pets

Unscramble the letters. Use the pictures to help you. Then, write the words on the lines.

a	c	t

_____

i	b	d	r

_____

s	f	h	i

_____

g	d	o

_____

Draw a picture of your pet or a pet you want.

Share Two Letters

Each word has two letters in common with the other words. Using the picture hints, fill in the rest of the words.

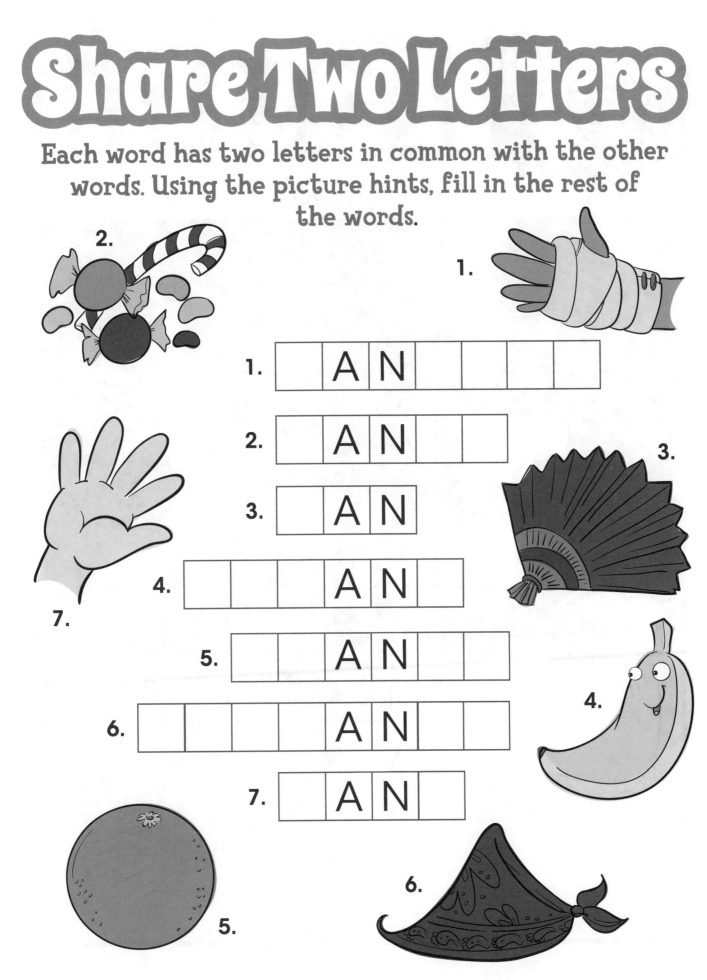

2.

1.

1. | | A | N | | | |

2. | | A | N | | |

3. | | A | N | | |

3.

4. | | | | A | N | |

5. | | | A | N | |

7.

6. | | | | | A | N | |

7. | | A | N | |

4.

6.

5.

What's

Can you spot and circle the

Different?

10 differences in these two pictures?

Rhyme This!

Using the pictures as hints, fill in the missing letters of the rhyming words.

		L	I	P

P	I	E

G	R	A	P	E

Share Two Letters

Each word has two letters in common with the other words. Using the picture hints, fill in the rest of the words.

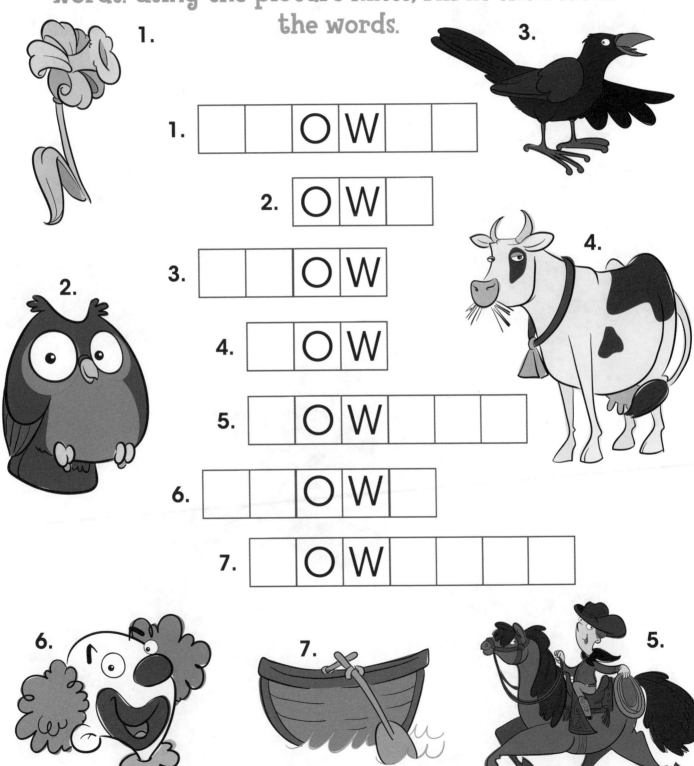

1. [ ] [ ] [O] [W] [ ]

2. [O] [W] [ ]

3. [ ] [ ] [O] [W]

4. [ ] [O] [W]

5. [ ] [O] [W] [ ] [ ] [ ]

6. [ ] [ ] [O] [W]

7. [ ] [O] [W] [ ] [ ] [ ]

WHAT'S THE DIFF?

One of these things is not like the others.
Can you find the imposter?

Rip-Roaring Rhymes

Using the pictures as hints, fill in the missing letters of the rhyming words.

F	L	O	A T

B	U	G

L	E	A	N

309

Share Two Letters

Each word has two letters in common with the other words. Using the picture hints, fill in the rest of the words.

2.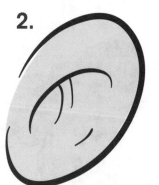

1.

1. `[ ] E A [ ]`

2. `E A [ ]`

3. `[ ] E A [ ]`

4. `[ ] E A [ ]`

5. `[ ] E A [ ]`

6. `[ ] E A [ ] [ ]`

7. `[ ] E A [ ] [ ]`

4.

3.

5.

7.

6.

NEW WORDS

Starting with the top word in each square, change one letter at a time until the top word becomes the bottom word.

C	A	P	E
F	I	N	S

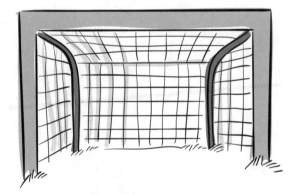

G	O	A	L
B	E	S	T

DIFFERENT?

10 differences in these two pictures?

For the Birds

Write the bird names from the word box in the puzzle.

1. | | a | |
2. | | | |
3. | | g | |
4. | | | |
5. | | | | t |
6. o | | | | |
7. | | e | | |
8. b | | | | |

buzzard ostrich eagle

jay robin owl

pigeons parrots

Super Spring

Read the clues and use the words in the word box to complete the puzzle.

butterfly	garden
umbrella	rain
March	sunflower
flowers	rainbow

Across

2. Water falling from the sky
4. Spring starts during this month.
5. A yellow flower that faces the sun
7. April showers bring May _____ .

Down

1. A caterpillar turns into a _____ .
2. Colorful arc in the sky after the rain
3. Hold this to stay dry when it rains
6. A place to plant flowers or plants

Camp Treasure Hunt

Find the **30** hidden items in the campsite next door.

- Ice Cream Cone
- Carrot
- Crescent Moon
- Cup with Straw
- Cheese Wedge
- Pencil
- Spoon
- Tea Cup
- Top Hat
- Donut
- Apple
- Fishhook
- Lollipop
- Smiley Face
- Paperclip
- Flag
- Arrow
- Party Hat
- Pizza Slice
- Turtle
- Pineapple
- Crown
- Heart
- Safari Helmet
- Leaf
- Sailboat
- Birdhouse
- Glove
- Toothbrush
- Bell

PICTURE CLUES

Use the pictures as clues to fill in the crossword puzzle.

1 ACROSS

2 ACROSS

1 DOWN

3 DOWN

4 DOWN

5 DOWN

6 ACROSS

7 ACROSS

318

PICTURE CLUES

Use the pictures as clues to fill in the crossword puzzle.

1 ACROSS

2 ACROSS

1 DOWN

3 DOWN

4 DOWN

5 DOWN

6 ACROSS

7 ACROSS

PUZZLE CLUES

Use the pictures as clues to fill in the crossword puzzle.

1 ACROSS

2 ACROSS

1 DOWN

3 DOWN

4 DOWN

5 DOWN

6 ACROSS

7 ACROSS

What's the Diff?

One of these things is not like the others.
Can you find the imposter?

LUNCH LINE TREASURE HUNT

Find the **24** hidden items in the cafeteria next door.

- ❑ Paintbrush
- ❑ Feather
- ❑ Arrow
- ❑ Lemon Slice
- ❑ Basketball
- ❑ Open Book
- ❑ Bowl
- ❑ Sailboat
- ❑ Donut
- ❑ Grapes
- ❑ Sock
- ❑ Crown
- ❑ Acorn
- ❑ Popsicle
- ❑ Heart
- ❑ Mitten
- ❑ Snowman
- ❑ Flag
- ❑ Spoon
- ❑ Music Note
- ❑ Rake
- ❑ Ice Cream Cone
- ❑ Ring
- ❑ Pencil

Woof!

Use the word lists to fill in the grid below.

Hint: Count the squares in the grid first to see where the words will fit.

3-Letters	4-Letters	5-Letters	6-Letters	7-Letters
sit	bone	leash	Beagle	Spaniel
toy	sled		Basset	
			collar	

Collie

Springtime

Use the word lists to fill in the grid below.

Hint: Count the squares in the grid first to see where the words will fit.

<u>3-Letters</u>
sun
May

<u>4-Letters</u>
root
warm
buds
rain

<u>5-Letters</u>
bloom
green
slush

<u>6-Letters</u>
flower
energy

s h o w e r s

LUAU!

Look at the pictures to complete the puzzle.

Across

2.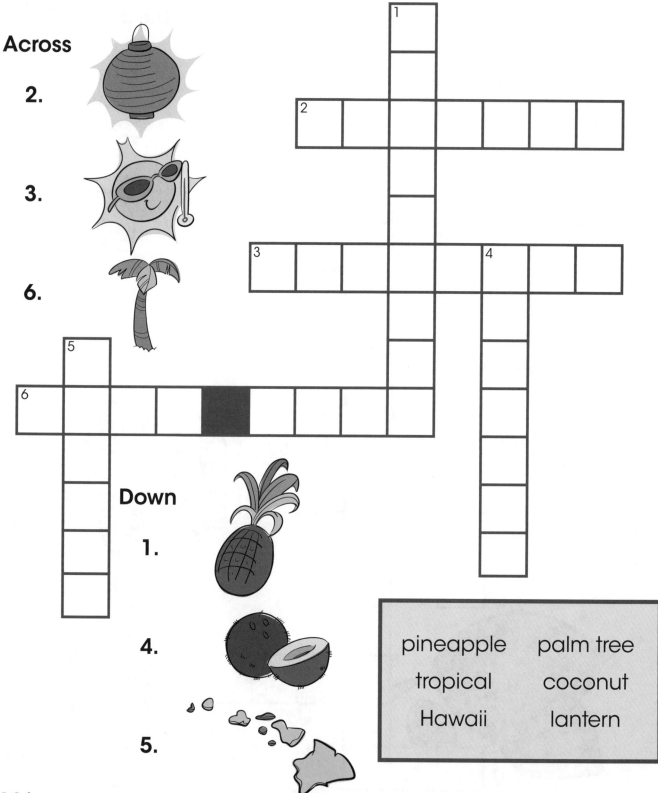

3.

6.

Down

1.

4.

5.

pineapple   palm tree
tropical   coconut
Hawaii   lantern

ZOMBIES & VAMPIRES

Print the first 8 letters of the alphabet in order in the boxes. Then, complete the name of each zombie or vampire using the word bank.

_ _ ☐ _ _ _ _

☐ _ _ _

☐ _ _ _ _ _

☐ _ _ _ _ _

_ _ ☐ _ _

☐ _ _ _ _

_ _ _ _ ☐ _ _

_ ☐ _ _ _

Word Bank
Crimson
Arachna
Fred
Merlin
Phantom
Blair
Twilight
Drusilla

Baker Treasure Hunt

Find the **32** hidden items in the bakery next door.

- ☐ Gift
- ☐ Lemon Slice
- ☐ Tree
- ☐ Crescent Moon
- ☐ Bowtie
- ☐ Candy Cane
- ☐ Paintbrush
- ☐ Top Hat
- ☐ Tea Cup
- ☐ Leaf
- ☐ Baseball Hat
- ☐ Ring
- ☐ Ruler
- ☐ Kite
- ☐ Comb
- ☐ Cup with Straw
- ☐ Shell
- ☐ Smiley Face
- ☐ Button
- ☐ Banana
- ☐ Flag
- ☐ Sailboat
- ☐ Lollipop
- ☐ Bucket
- ☐ Pencil
- ☐ Heart
- ☐ Birdhouse
- ☐ Worm
- ☐ Basketball
- ☐ Mushroom
- ☐ Ladybug
- ☐ Arrow

Compound Fun

Match each word in the word box with a word in the puzzle to make a new word.

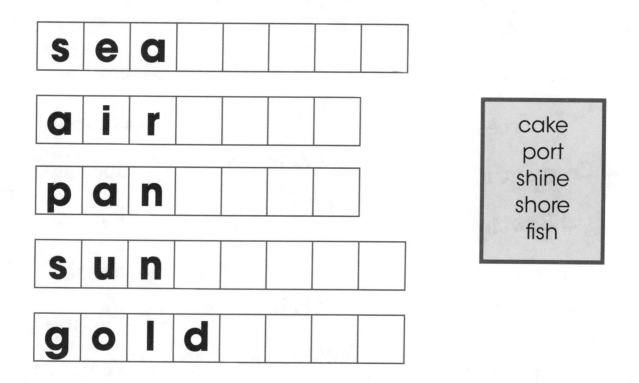

| s | e | a | | | | |

| a | i | r | | | | |

| p | a | n | | | | |

| s | u | n | | | | |

| g | o | l | d | | | |

cake
port
shine
shore
fish

Magnificent Monet

Read the clues and use the words in the word box to complete the puzzle.

France

water lilies

Notre Dame

Paris

painter

bonjour

Across
4. Capital city of France
5. Famous cathedral in France
6. Monet's profession or job

Down
1. Monet's home
2. How the French say hello
3. Flowers located in a pond; title of a Monet painting

Answer Key

7

8

10

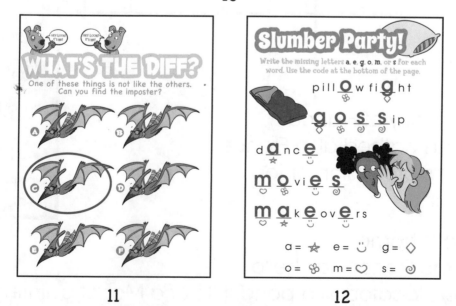

11   12

Answer Key

SILLY ANIMALS

Below are some silly pictures made from animals put together. Write the names of the two real mammals suggested by the picture.
Then, draw your own silly animal!

1. elephant
2. camel

1. kangaroo
2. skunk

1. raccoon
2. zebra

Drawings will vary.

13

Different?

10 differences in these two pictures?

15

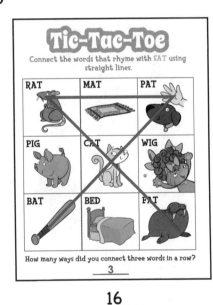

Tic-Tac-Toe

Connect the words that rhyme with SAT using straight lines.

RAT	MAT	PAT
PIG	CAT	WIG
BAT	BED	FAT

How many ways did you connect three words in a row?

3

16

AMERICANIZE

Read the sentences below. Use the word bank to find and write the words Americans might use for the Australian expressions in bold.

Word Bank
faucets
trunk
hood
gasoline

We need to add **petrol** gasoline to the automobile.

The attendant checked under the **bonnet** hood as I arranged things in the **boot** trunk of the car.

Sidney is located near the mouth of a river to provide water for the **taps** faucets .

17

Secret Code

Write the letter for each symbol. Use the code at the bottom of the page.

What happened when the Easter Bunny told a bunch of silly jokes?

A L L O F

T H E E G G S

C R A C K E D

U P

| L | A | F | O | E | T | H | G |
| S | C | K | R | D | P | U | |

18

Answer Key

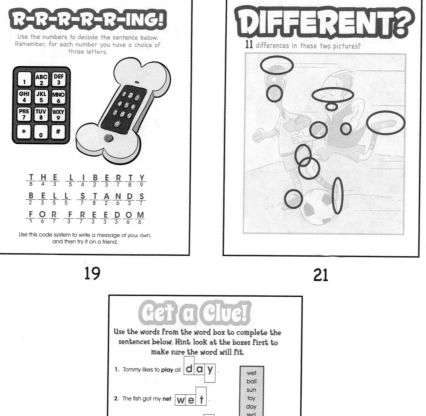

19

21

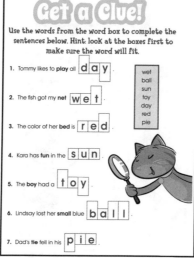

22

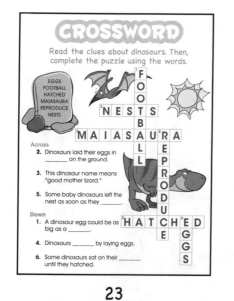

23

24

Answer Key

Sunshine

How many words can you make from the letters in SUNSHINE?

SUN _____   HIS _____

Answers will vary.

26

SPELLING AS

Use the clues and the word bank to help you. Write these words like PT would.

A boy named PT likes to take shortcuts when he has a lot to write. He will show U an EZ way to spell. B prepared to B the NV of all your friends. RU ready?

1. A kind of tent — **TP**

 tepee TP

2. An insect — **B**

3. A hot drink — **T**

4. A vegetable — **P**

5. A question word — **Y**

6. A banana's skin — **PL**

7. A word that means slippery — **IC**

Word Bank
bee
icy
why
peel
pea
tea
tepee

27

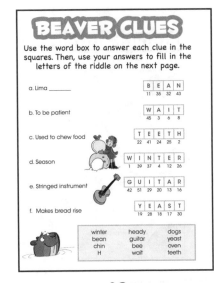

BEAVER CLUES

Use the word box to answer each clue in the squares. Then, use your answers to fill in the letters of the riddle on the next page.

a. Lima _____   B E A N
                    11 35 32 43

b. To be patient   W A I T
                    45 3 6 8

c. Used to chew food   T E E T H
                        22 41 24 25 2

d. Season   W I N T E R
             1 39 37 4 12 26

e. Stringed instrument   G U I T A R
                          42 51 29 20 13 16

f. Makes bread rise   Y E A S T
                       19 28 18 17 30

winter	heady	dogs
bean	guitar	yeast
chin	bee	oven
H	wait	teeth

28

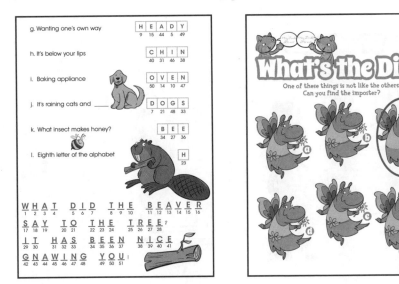

g. Wanting one's own way   H E A D Y
                            9 15 44 5 49

h. It's below your lips   C H I N
                           40 31 46 38

i. Baking appliance   O V E N
                       50 14 10 47

j. It's raining cats and _____   D O G S
                                  7 21 48 33

k. What insect makes honey?   B E E
                               34 27 36

l. Eighth letter of the alphabet   H
                                    23

W H A T   D I D   T H E   B E A V E R
1 2 3 4   5 6 7   8 9 10 11 12 13 14 15 16

S A Y   T O   T H E   T R E E ?
17 18 19 20 21 22 23 24 25 26 27 28

I T   H A S   B E E N   N I C E
29 30 31 32 33 34 35 36 37 38 39 40 41

G N A W I N G   Y O U !
42 43 44 45 46 47 48 49 50 51

29

What's the Diff?

One of these things is not like the others. Can you find the imposter?

a   b   c

d   e   f

30

Answer Key

ANIMAL CLUES

Read the clues and use the words in the word box to complete the puzzle.

chinchilla	kangaroo rat
emperor penguin	tarantula
gnu	yak

¹K
²C H I N C H I L L A
A
N
G
³T A R A N T U L A
A
R
O
⁵E M P O R O R P E N G U I N
R N
T U
⁴Y A K

Down
1. I can save unchewed food in my stomach and later return it to my mouth for a meal.
2. "What's new?" I'm often asked. I only shake my head and smile.

Across
3. While some may desire my coat, I need it more then they.
4. Things may become a bit "hairy" if I crawl near you.
5. Who needs a president when I'm titled for life?
6. I can't talk, although my name may indicate the contrary.

31

32

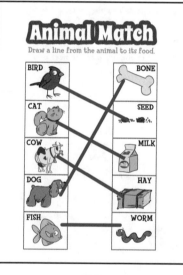

Animal Match

Draw a line from the animal to its food.

BIRD — BONE
CAT — SEED
COW — MILK
DOG — HAY
FISH — WORM

34

EASY AS ABC

Use the clues and the word bank to help you write more words like PT would.

tepee TP

1. Pass cards to players   DL
2. Nothing in it   MT
3. A girl's name   KT
4. Pep   NRG
5. I am, he is, you   R
6. A bird that is blue   J

Word Bank
are
empty
energy
Katie
deal
jay

35

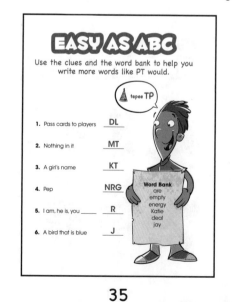

36

Answer Key

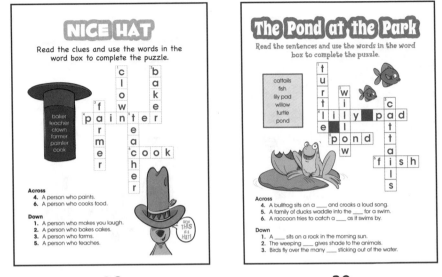

NICE HAT

Read the clues and use the words in the word box to complete the puzzle.

Word box: baker, teacher, clown, farmer, painter, cook

Puzzle answers:
- clown
- baker
- farmer
- painter
- teacher
- cook

Across
4. A person who paints.
6. A person who cooks food.

Down
1. A person who makes you laugh.
2. A person who bakes cakes.
3. A person who farms.
5. A person who teaches.

NOW THIS IS A HAT!

38

The Pond at the Park

Read the sentences and use the words in the word box to complete the puzzle.

Word box: cattails, fish, lily pad, willow, turtle, pond

Puzzle answers:
- turtle
- willow
- lily pad
- cattails
- pond
- fish

Across
4. A bullfrog sits on a _____ and croaks a loud song.
5. A family of ducks waddle into the _____ for a swim.
6. A raccoon tries to catch a _____ as it swims by.

Down
1. A _____ sits on a rock in the morning sun.
2. The weeping _____ gives shade to the animals.
3. Birds fly over the many _____ sticking out of the water.

39

40

Sea Turtles

How many words can you make from the letters in SEA TURTLES?

TALE   RAT

Answers will vary.

42

HOT STUFF

Each rebus stands for a word listed in the word bank. Help the knight solve the puzzle by writing one word on each line. You will have to respell some words.

1. H + 🫖 - P
2. 🧂 + S
3. ✋ - H
4. CH + 🦈 - GL + I
5. 🔥
6. 🥧 - AT
7. 👁 - C

Word Bank
hot
me
peppers
and
up
fire
chili

Hot   peppers
and   chili   fire
me   up   !

43

337

Answer Key

44

45

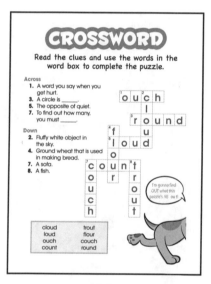

46

47

48

Answer Key

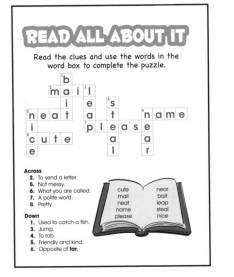

READ ALL ABOUT IT

Read the clues and use the words in the word box to complete the puzzle.

Across
2. To send a letter.
5. Not messy.
6. What you are called.
7. A polite word.
8. Pretty.

Down
1. Used to catch a fish.
3. Jump.
4. To rob.
5. Friendly and kind.
6. Opposite of **far**.

cute   near
mail   bait
neat   leap
name   steal
please   nice

50

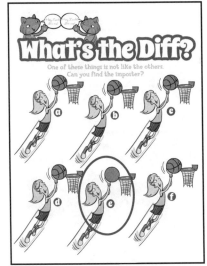

What's the Diff?

One of these things is not like the others. Can you find the imposter?

51

Secret Code

Decode the message using the symbols below.

C A T

F I S H I N G !

A B C D E F G H I J K L M

N O P Q R S T U V W X Y Z

52

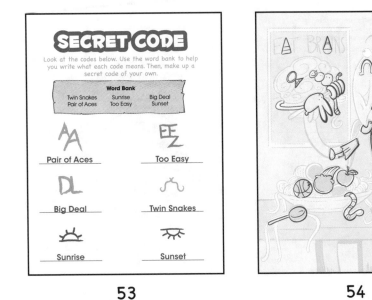

SECRET CODE

Look at the codes below. Use the word bank to help you write what each code means. Then, make up a secret code of your own.

Word Bank

Twin Snakes   Sunrise   Big Deal
Pair of Aces   Too Easy   Sunset

Pair of Aces

Too Easy

Big Deal

Twin Snakes

Sunrise

Sunset

53

54

339

Answer Key

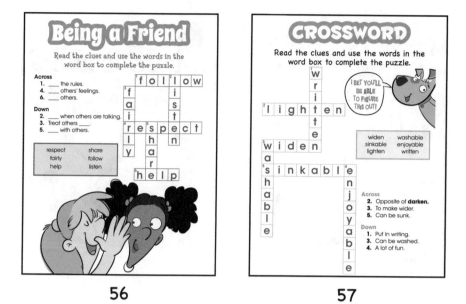

Being a Friend

Read the clues and use the words in the word box to complete the puzzle.

Across
1. _____ the rules.
4. _____ others' feelings.
6. _____ others.

Down
2. _____ when others are talking.
3. Treat others _____.
5. _____ with others.

Puzzle answers:
- follow
- fist / fairly
- respect
- share
- help

Word box:
respect   share
fairly   follow
help   listen

56

CROSSWORD

Read the clues and use the words in the word box to complete the puzzle.

I BET YOU'LL BE ABLE TO FIGURE THIS OUT!

Puzzle answers:
- written
- lighten
- widen
- washable
- sinkable
- enjoyable

Word box:
widen   washable
sinkable   enjoyable
lighten   written

Across
2. Opposite of **darken.**
3. To make wider.
5. Can be sunk.

Down
1. Put in writing.
3. Can be washed.
4. A lot of fun.

57

DIFFERENT?

10 differences in these two pictures?

59

RIDDLE TIME

Use the word box on the next page to answer each clue in the squares on the right. Then, use your answers to fill in the letters of the riddle on the next page.

a. Not old

Y	O	U	N	G
38	34	40	25	48

b. _____ and thank you

P	L	E	A	S	E
45	42	20	14	32	7

c. Police _____

S	T	A	T	I	O	N
41	9	24	4	46	11	15

d. Tells the time

W	A	T	C	H
1	35	33	13	2

e. You smell with this

N	O	S	E
19	17	26	22

f. Long stream of water

R	I	V	E	R
23	10	21	37	36

g. Female nobility

Q	U	E	E	N
5	6	31	44	47

60

h. What you do with a paddle

R	O	W
29	39	27

i. Japanese currency

Y	E	N
30	28	12

j. You don't _____? (rhymes with "hay")

S	A	Y
8	3	16

k. Second and last vowels in the alphabet, not including "y"

E	U
43	18

Word box:
watch   please
river   EU
yen   nose
young   station
queen   say
row

WHAT QUESTION CAN
1 2 3 4 5 6 7 8 9 10 11 12 13 14 15

YOU NEVER ANSWER
16 17 18 19 20 21 22 23 24 25 26 27 28 29

YES TO?
30 31 32 33 34

ARE YOU SLEEPING?
35 36 37 38 39 40 41 42 43 44 45 46 47 48

61

340

Answer Key

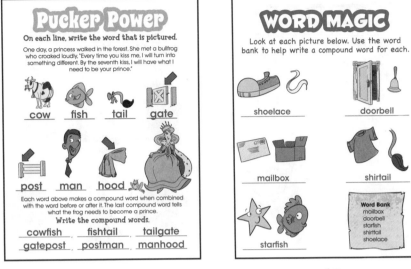

62

63

65

66

67

Answer Key

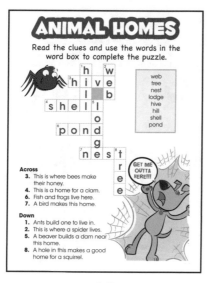

ANIMAL HOMES

Read the clues and use the words in the word box to complete the puzzle.

Word box: web, tree, nest, lodge, hive, hill, shell, pond

Crossword answers:
- h i v e
- h i l l
- s h e l l
- p o n d
- n e s t
- (down words): web, lodge, tree

Across
3. This is where bees make their honey.
4. This is a home for a clam.
6. Fish and frogs live here.
7. A bird makes this home.

Down
1. Ants build one to live in.
2. This is where a spider lives.
5. A beaver builds a dam near this home.
8. A hole in this makes a good home for a squirrel.

GET ME OUTTA HERE!!!

68

What's the Diff?

One of these things is not like the others. Can you find the imposter?

a b c
d e f

(d is circled)

69

70

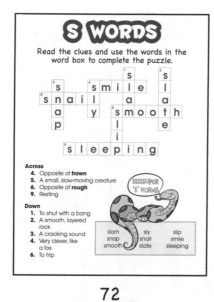

S WORDS

Read the clues and use the words in the word box to complete the puzzle.

Crossword answers:
- s m i l e
- s n a i l
- s m o o t h
- s l e e p i n g

Across
4. Opposite of **frown**
5. A small, slow-moving creature
6. Opposite of **rough**
9. Resting

Down
1. To shut with a bang
2. A smooth, layered rock
3. A cracking sound
4. Very clever, like a fox
6. To trip

SSSSSUPER "S" WORDS!

Word box: slam, snap, smooth, sly, snail, slate, slip, smile, sleeping

72

Butterfly

How many words can you make from the letters in BUTTERFLY?

FRY ____   TUB ____

Answers will vary.

73

342

Answer Key

Five Senses

Read the clues and use the words in the word box to complete the puzzle.

```
t o u c h
a      e y e s
s      a   a
t      r   r
       s   s
s m e l l
o
u
t
h a n d s
```

Word box:
eyes
hear
ears
taste
mouth
touch
hands
smell

Across
1. Your hands help you do this.
3. You look at a pretty butterfly with these.
5. You use your nose to do this to a flower.
6. You use these to touch a soft kitten.

Down
1. Your mouth helps you do this.
2. Your ears help you do this.
4. You listen to music with these.
7. You taste your favorite fruit with this.

74

PUPPY POWER

Complete these five sentences. Then, use the words you wrote to answer the question.

Big is to **small** as **day** is to **night**. (Words are opposites.)
Robin is to **bird** as **spaniel** is to **dog**. (Kind of bird; kind of dog)

1. **Here** is to **there** as **then** is to ___now___.
2. **Tack** is to **stack** as **pot** is to ___spot___.
3. **Net** is to **ten** as **saw** is to ___was___.
4. **Down** is to **up** as **bottom** is to ___top___.
5. **Siamese** is to **cat** as **poodle** is to ___dog___.

Why was the spotted dog happy?

___Now___ ___Spot___ ___was___

___top___ ___dog___.

75

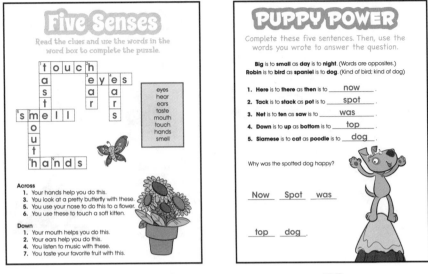

76

Springtime

Read the clues and use the words in the word box to complete the puzzle.

Word box:
chick
shower
think
shade
thirteen
white

```
       w h i t e
       h
    c h i c k
       r
       t h i n k
       e
  s h o w e r
  h    e
  a    n
  d
  e
```

Across
1. Clouds can be this color.
3. This hatches from an egg.
4. You do this with your brain.
5. It is a spray of water.

Down
2. The number after twelve.
5. You may find this under a tree.

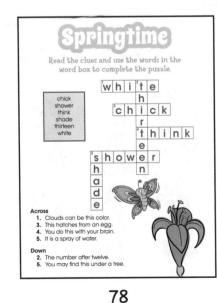

78

WINTER

Read the clues and use the words in the word box to complete the puzzle.

```
       s l e e p
       n
  s h o v e l
  k    w
  i    m
  s    a
       i n d o o r s
```

Word box:
snowman
skis
sleep
indoors
shovel

Across
1. This is what some animals do in winter.
2. Use this to take the snow off of sidewalks.
3. This is where to stay warm in a snowstorm.

Down
1. You can build one in the snow.
2. Wear two of them on your feet.

79

Answer Key

80

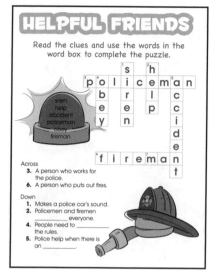

82

83

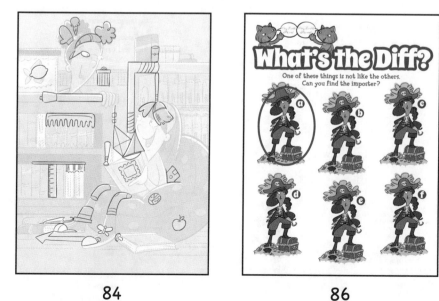

84   86

Answer Key

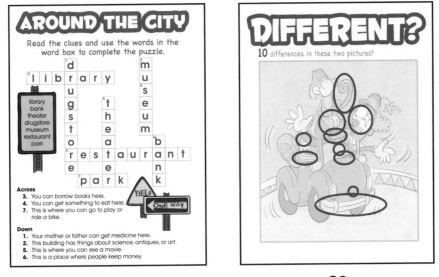

AROUND THE CITY

Read the clues and use the words in the word box to complete the puzzle.

Word box: library, bank, theater, drugstore, museum, restaurant, park

Crossword answers:
- 3. library
- 4. restaurant
- 7. park
- 1. drugstore
- 2. museum
- 5. theater
- 6. bank

Across
3. You can borrow books here.
4. You can get something to eat here.
7. This is where you can go to play or ride a bike.

Down
1. Your mother or father can get medicine here.
2. This building has things about science, antiques, or art.
5. This is where you can see a movie.
6. This is a place where people keep money.

87

DIFFERENT?

10 differences in these two pictures?

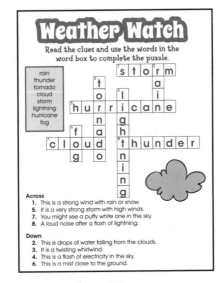

89

Weather Watch

Read the clues and use the words in the word box to complete the puzzle.

Word box: rain, thunder, tornado, cloud, storm, lightning, hurricane, fog

Crossword answers:
- 1. storm
- 5. hurricane
- 7. cloud
- 8. thunder
- 2. rain
- 3. tornado
- 4. lightning
- 6. fog

Across
1. This is a strong wind with rain or snow.
5. It is a very strong storm with high winds.
7. You might see a puffy white one in the sky.
8. A loud noise after a flash of lightning.

Down
2. This is drops of water falling from the clouds.
3. It is a twisting whirlwind.
4. This is a flash of electricity in the sky.
6. This is a mist close to the ground.

90

AT SCHOOL

Read the clues and use the words in the word box to complete the puzzle.

Word box: teacher, children, computer, read, write, learn

Crossword answers:
- 1. computer
- 4. write
- 5. teacher
- 1. children
- 2. read
- 6. learn

Across
1. This is a machine that helps you learn.
4. You do this with a pencil or a computer.
5. This is a person who helps you learn.

Down
1. These are young people who go to school.
2. This is what you do with a book.
6. This means **to find out about things**.

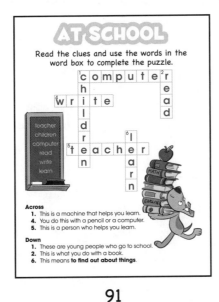

91

Different?

10 differences in these two pictures?

93

345

Answer Key

Kitten Family

How many words can you make from the letters in KITTEN FAMILY?

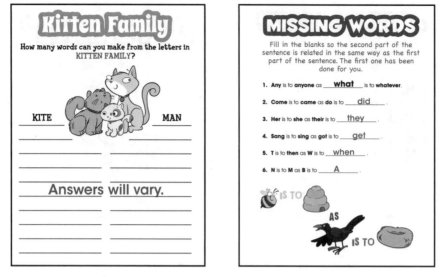

KITE   MAN

Answers will vary.

94

MISSING WORDS

Fill in the blanks so the second part of the sentence is related in the same way as the first part of the sentence. The first one has been done for you.

1. **Any** is to **anyone** as ___**what**___ is to **whatever**.
2. **Come** is to **came** as **do** is to ___**did**___.
3. **Her** is to **she** as **their** is to ___**they**___.
4. **Sang** is to **sing** as **got** is to ___**get**___.
5. **T** is to **then** as **W** is to ___**when**___.
6. **N** is to **M** as **B** is to ___**A**___.

IS TO
AS
IS TO

95

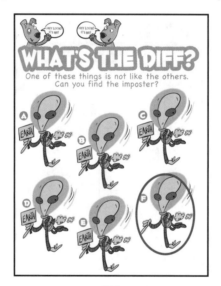

96

Bookworm

Read the clues and use the words in the word box to complete the puzzle.

title
author
illustrator
date
words
pictures
cover

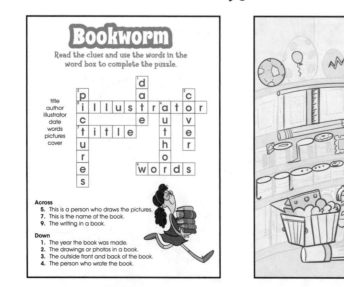

Across
5. This is a person who draws the pictures.
7. This is the name of the book.
9. The writing in a book.

Down
1. The year the book was made.
2. The drawings or photos in a book.
3. The outside front and back of the book.
4. The person who wrote the book.

97

98

Answer Key

100

PIG PEN

Use the word box to answer each clue in the squares. Then, use your answers to fill in the letters of the riddle on the next page.

a. Makes you say, "Ouch!"
P A I N
8 3 9 12

b. Class where you learn to add
M A T H
25 11 4 32

c. Where bees live
H I V E
17 14 19 41

d. Hospital room with a TV and magazines
W A I T I N G
1 7 21 31 34 42 10

e. You bake it in
O V E N
30 35 20 22

f. Piggy _____
B A N K
29 18 38 16

110

101

g. Swimming place
P O O L
40 24 27 33

h. Opposite of "subtract"
A D D
39 5 13

i. It lays eggs
H E N
2 36 28

j. A penny is a _____
C O I N
23 6 37 15

k. Thirteenth letter of the alphabet
M
26

coin	hen
hive	math
bank	M
pain	add
pool	waiting
oven	

W H A T   D O   A   P I G   A N D
1 2 3 4   5 6   7   8 9 10   11 12 13

I N K   H A V E   I N   C O M M O N ?
14 15 16   17 18 19 20   21 22   23 24 25 26 27 28

B O T H   L I V E   I N   A   P E N
29 30 31 32   33 34 35 36   37 38   39   40 41 42

102

Slumber Party!

Unscramble the words and write them on the lines.

wlpiol **p i l l o w**

sgpios **g o s s i p**

mgeas **g a m e s**

vsoiem **m o v i e s**

esligpen agb

s l e e p i n g   b a g

103

SCRAMBLE

Use the words in the word bank to write the missing words in the sentences. Then, unscramble the letters in the circles to find out what Stegosaurus liked to eat.

Stegosaurus had a small **h e (a) d**.

Stegosaurus had sharp **s (p) i k e s** on the end of its tail.

Stegosaurus was about 25 **f e e (t)** long.

Stegosaurus weighed over 3 **t o n (s)**.

Stegosaurus had bony **p (l) a t e s** on its back.

Its head was close to the **g r o u (n) d**.

| plates |
| spikes |
| ground |
| head |
| tons |
| feet |

Stegosaurus ate **p l a n t s**.

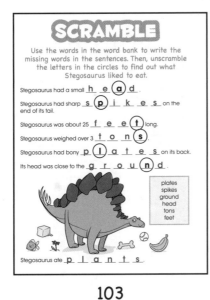

104

347

Answer Key

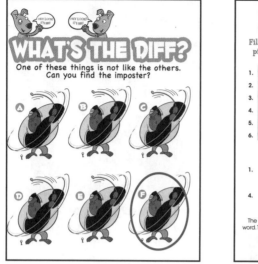

106

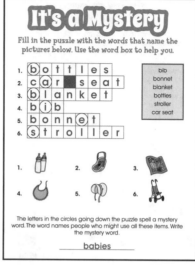

It's a Mystery

Fill in the puzzle with the words that name the pictures below. Use the word box to help you.

1. b o t t l e s
2. c a r   s e a t
3. b l a n k e t
4. b i b
5. b o n n e t
6. s t r o l l e r

Word box:
bib
bonnet
blanket
bottles
stroller
car seat

The letters in the circles going down the puzzle spell a mystery word. The word names people who might use all these items. Write the mystery word.

babies

107

108

Sweet Spring

Read the clues and use the words in the word box to complete the puzzle.

¹c
²w a r m e r
a
³f l o w e r s
u   r
t   p
d   i
o   ⁵w
o   i   ⁶k i t e
r   l   n
s   l   d
a
⁷r a i n y

Word box:
warmer
flowers
caterpillar
windy
rainy
kite
outdoors

Across
2. It is the opposite of **colder**.
3. These bloom in the spring.
6. You can fly one outdoors in the spring.
7. Take your umbrella on days like this.

Down
1. This is busy eating new leaves in spring.
4. It's fun to play here.
5. This is a good day to fly a kite.

109

Different?

10 differences in these two pictures?

111

348

Answer Key

Spa Party!
Unscramble the words and write them on the lines.

nrmeacui <u>m a n i c u r e</u>

varkmeoe <u>m a k e o v e r</u>

deipurce <u>p e d i c u r e</u>

filaca <u>f a c i a l</u>

smasega <u>m a s s a g e</u>

112

APATOSAURUS
Create a rhyme about Apatosaurus. Fill in each blank using the information given.

Its neck was long.

Its bones were <u>s t r o n g</u>.

It reached with ease to the tops of <u>t r e e s</u>.

Its skin was <u>t o u g h</u>.

And that's enough!

113

WHAT'S THE DIFF?
One of these things is not like the others. Can you find the imposter?

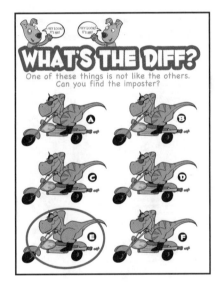

114

FALL
Read the clues and use the words in the word box to complete the puzzle.

Word box: leaves, pumpkin, apples, moon, yellow, squirrels, geese, rake

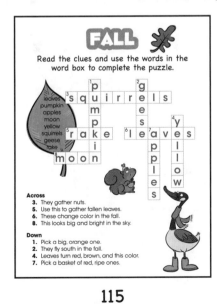

Across
3. They gather nuts.
5. Use this to gather fallen leaves.
6. These change color in the fall.
8. This looks big and bright in the sky.

Down
1. Pick a big, orange one.
2. They fly south in the fall.
4. Leaves turn red, brown, and this color.
7. Pick a basket of red, ripe ones.

115

What's the Diff?
One of these things is not like the others. Can you find the imposter?

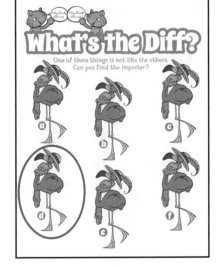

116

349

Answer Key

117

118

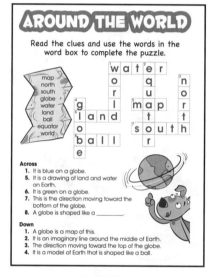

119

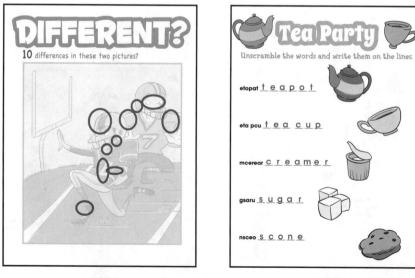

121

122

Answer Key

MAIL CALL

Unscramble the words that have to do with mail. Use the words in the word bank to help you.

rettles — l e t t e r s
cpageksa — p a c k a g e s
axombli — m a i l b o x
leeydivr — d e l i v e r y
dracs — c a r d s

Word bank:
delivery
letters
mailbox
cards
packages

Draw a picture of your favorite thing to receive in the mail.

Drawings will vary.

123

WHAT'S THE DIFF?

One of these things is not like the others. Can you find the imposter?

(Circle around C)

124

Making Music

Read the clues and use the words in the word box to complete the puzzle.

Word box:
drum
horn
violin
piano
guitar
note
music
listen

Across
3. This instrument has black and white keys.
5. It is a musical sound.
6. You blow into this instrument.
7. Strike this instrument to make sounds.

Down
1. You play the strings on this instrument with a bow.
2. People do this when they hear music.
4. An electric one is used for rock and roll.
8. It is another word for **beautiful sounds**.

125

126

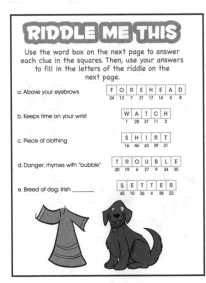

RIDDLE ME THIS

Use the word box on the next page to answer each clue in the squares. Then, use your answers to fill in the letters of the riddle on the next page.

a. Above your eyebrows — F O R E H E A D
   24 12 7 21 17 14 3 8

b. Keeps time on your wrist — W A T C H
   1 28 37 11 2

c. Piece of clothing — S H I R T
   16 46 43 39 31

d. Danger; rhymes with "bubble" — T R O U B L E
   20 19 6 27 9 34 35

e. Breed of dog; Irish _____ — S E T T E R
   45 10 36 4 38 22

128

Answer Key

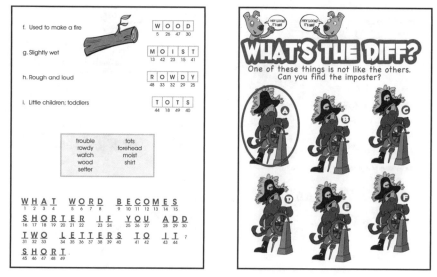

f. Used to make a fire — W O O D (5 26 47 30)

g. Slightly wet — M O I S T (13 42 23 15 41)

h. Rough and loud — R O W D Y (48 33 32 29 25)

i. Little children; toddlers — T O T S (44 18 49 40)

trouble	tots
rowdy	forehead
watch	moist
wood	shirt
setter	

W H A T W O R D B E C O M E S
1 2 3   4 5 6 7 8   9 10 11 12 13 14 15

S H O R T E R I F Y O U A D D
16 17 18 19 20 21 22   23 24   25 26 27   28 29 30

T W O L E T T E R S T O I T ?
31 32 33   34 35 36 37 38 39 40   41 42   43 44

S H O R T.
45 46 47 48 49

129

WHAT'S THE DIFF?

One of these things is not like the others.
Can you find the imposter?

130

PLACES, EVERYONE!

Use the word bank and the pictures below to help
you fill in the puzzle. Use the order of the pictures as
clues. The first one has been done for you.

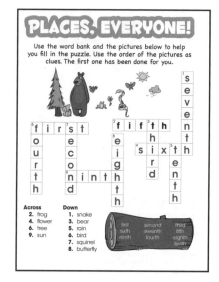

Across
2. frog
4. flower
6. tree
9. sun

Down
1. snake
3. bear
5. rain
6. bird
7. squirrel
8. butterfly

131

What's the Diff?

One of these things is not like the others.
Can you find the imposter?

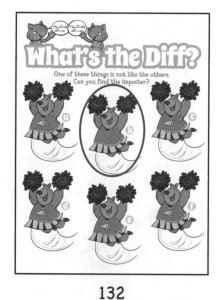

132

Facing the Sun

Read the clues and use the words in the
word box to complete the puzzle.

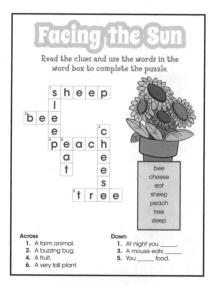

bee
cheese
eat
sheep
peach
tree
sleep

Across
1. A farm animal.
2. A buzzing bug.
4. A fruit.
6. A very tall plant.

Down
1. At night you _____.
3. A mouse eats _____.
5. You _____ food.

133

Answer Key

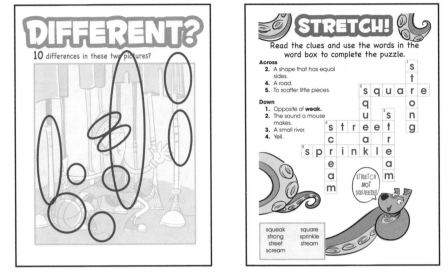

135

STRETCH!

Read the clues and use the words in the word box to complete the puzzle.

Across
2. A shape that has equal sides.
4. A road.
5. To scatter little pieces.

Down
1. Opposite of **weak.**
2. The sound a mouse makes.
3. A small river.
4. Yell.

						s
		s	q	u	a	r	e
		q		s		r	
	s	t	r	e	e	t	
		e		c		o	
s	p	r	i	n	k	l	e
		a		r		n	
		m		e		g	
				a			
				m			

STRETCH NOT SQUEEZE!

squeak square
strong sprinkle
street stream
scream

136

137

PRESIDENTS

The names of 5 of America's past presidents have been scrambled below. Each name also has a clue to help you identify the president.

Write each name. Use the word bank.

REGGEO GSWOAHNITN   **George Washington**
The father of our country

HOJN SMAAD   **John Adams**
The first president to live in the White House

MABRAAH CNILLON   **Abraham Lincoln**
Freed the slaves

KNIRFALN SERVOTLOE   **Franklin Roosevelt**
Served four times as president

LANROD GRANEA   **Ronald Reagan**
Had been a movie star

Word Bank
Ronald Reagan
John Adams
George Washington
Abraham Lincoln
Franklin Roosevelt

138

Word Match

Read the two words on each animal. If they have about the same meaning, color the animal brown. If they do not have the same meaning, color the animal red.

139

353

Answer Key

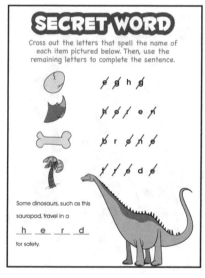

140

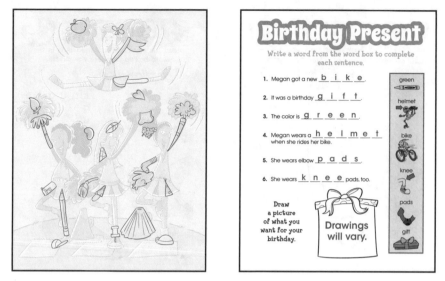

Birthday Present

Write a word from the word box to complete each sentence.

1. Megan got a new b i k e .
2. It was a birthday g i f t .
3. The color is g r e e n .
4. Megan wears a h e l m e t when she rides her bike.
5. She wears elbow p a d s .
6. She wears k n e e pads, too.

Draw a picture of what you want for your birthday.

Drawings will vary.

green
helmet
bike
knee
pads
gift

142

SECRET WORD

Cross out the letters that spell the name of each item pictured below. Then, use the remaining letters to complete the sentence.

e g h g

h o e n

b r o h e

t t e d e

Some dinosaurs, such as this sauropod, travel in a

h e r d

for safety.

143

WHAT'S THE DIFF?

One of these things is not like the others. Can you find the imposter?

A   B   C

D   E   F

144

CAREER TIME

Use the pictures and words in the word box to help you fill in the puzzle.

1. c h e f
2. d o c t o r
3. a r t i s t
4. l a w y e r
5. t e a c h e r
6. s i n g e r

doctor
teacher
artist
lawyer
singer
chef

1.   2.   3.

4. I OBJECT!   5.   6.

145

Answer Key

146

Soooo...Cozy

Read the clues and use the words in the word box to complete the puzzle.

Word box:
bones stove
boat home
open road
hole notes

Across
3. Not shut
5. Dogs like these.
7. A street

Down
1. Your house
2. A mole digs this.
4. Musical
5. A ship
6. You cook on this.

148

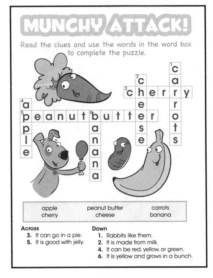

MUNCHY ATTACK!

Read the clues and use the words in the word box to complete the puzzle.

Word box:
apple peanut butter carrots
cherry cheese banana

Across
3. It can go in a pie.
5. It is good with jelly.

Down
1. Rabbits like them.
2. It is made from milk.
4. It can be red, yellow, or green.
6. It is yellow and grows in a bunch.

149

Awesome Accessories

Unscramble the accessories and write them on the lines.

kneeaclc __n e c k l a c e__

fcsra __s c a r f__

rpues __p u r s e__

trcablee __b r a c e l e t__

nigr __r i n g__

150

WHEEL OF NOUNS

Try your hand at creating a "wheel of nouns."

1. Begin with the word *cat*.
2. Continue clockwise around the circle by adding a word that is spelled like the previous word except for one letter. Use the picture clues.
3. Make sure that the last word you choose can again turn into the first word with a one-letter change.

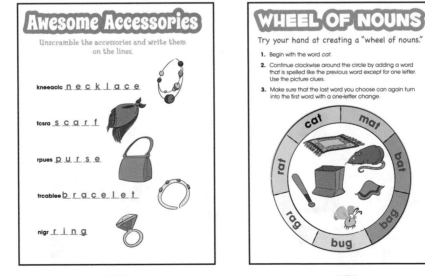

cat mat bat bag bug rag rat

151

Answer Key

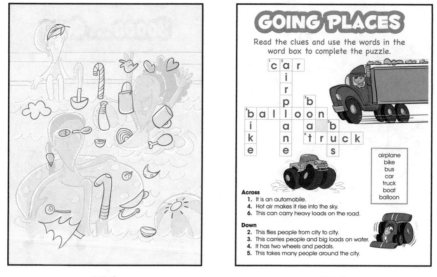

152

154

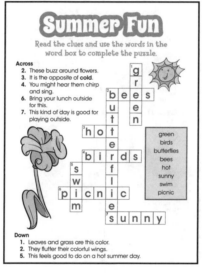

155

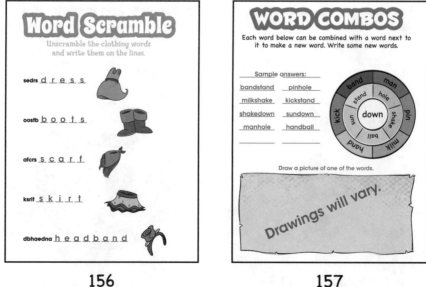

156

157

Answer Key

158

160

161

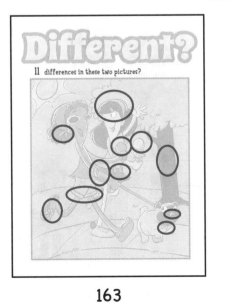

163

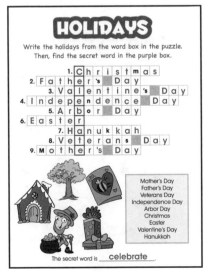

164

Answer Key

Calendar Clues

Read the clues and use the words in the word box to complete the puzzle.

Word box: days, week, month, year, calendar, holiday, birthday, time

Crossword grid:
- 1 Down: b
- 2 Across: h o l i d a y (with i, r, t, h, d, a, y going down as birthday)
- 3 Across: t i m e
- 4 Across: m o n t h
- 5 Down: w e e k
- 6 Across: c a l e n d a r
- 7 Down: d a y s
- 8 Across: y e a r

Across
2. It is a day for celebrating instead of working.
3. It can be measured in days, weeks, months, and years.
4. It can have 28 to 31 days.
6. You can hang it on a wall to keep track of the days.
8. This has twelve months.

Down
1. This is the day you were born.
5. It has seven days.
7. A year has 365 of these.

165

Number This!

Unscramble and write the number words.

nnei   n i n e
neves   s e v e n
wetlev   t w e l v e
etreh   t h r e e
xis   s i x
etn   t e n

Word box: three, six, seven, nine, ten, twelve

166

FUNNY FOOD FACTS

Read each sentence. Cross out the noun that doesn't make sense. Find a noun in another sentence that fits but still makes a silly sentence. Write it above the crossed-out word. The first one has been done for you.

1. Lazy people eat ~~chili~~ **meatloaf**.
2. The Easter Bunny's favorite vegetables are ~~chicken~~ **jellybeans**.
3. The best fruit to drink is ~~strawberries~~ **watermelon**.
4. If you're scared, don't eat ~~dough~~ **chicken**.
5. ~~Jellybeans~~ **Chili** must be a cold food.
6. Dancing cows make ~~blueberries~~ **milkshakes**.
7. Cavemen ate ~~meatloaf~~ **club sandwiches**.
8. Bread is rich because it has ~~watermelon~~ **dough**.
9. ~~Milkshakes~~ **Blueberries** are an unhappy fruit.
10. ~~Club sandwiches~~ **Strawberries** grow on the floor of a barn.

167

DIFFERENT?

10 differences in these two pictures?

169

BRRR!

Use the word lists to fill out the grid below. Hint: Count the squares in the grid first to see where the words will fit.

3-Letters	4-Letters	5-Letters	6-Letters	7-Letters
ice	cold	sleet	skated	shivers
ski	melt	spill		
		parka		

Grid:
- s
- s p i l l, l
- h, e
- m i t t e n s
- v, t, k
- m e l t, p a r k a
- r, t
- s k i, e
- c o l d
- e

170

358

Answer Key

171 — Love Day

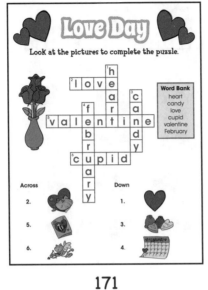

Look at the pictures to complete the puzzle.

Crossword:
- 2 Across: love
- 5 Across: valentine
- 6 Across: cupid
- 1 Down: heart
- 3 Down: candy
- 4 Down: february

Word Bank
heart
candy
love
cupid
valentine
February

Across
2.
5.
6.

Down
1.
3.
4.

172 — Number This!

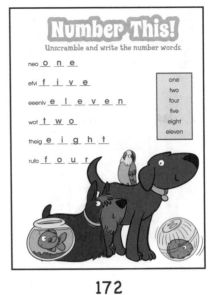

Unscramble and write the number words.

neo — o n e
efvi — f i v e
eeenlv — e l e v e n
wot — t w o
theig — e i g h t
rufo — f o u r

Word box:
one
two
four
five
eight
eleven

173 — HOME SWEET HOME

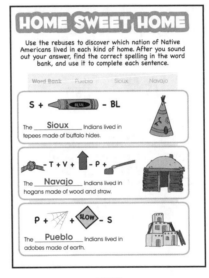

Use the rebuses to discover which nation of Native Americans lived in each kind of home. After you sound out your answer, find the correct spelling in the word bank, and use it to complete each sentence.

Word Bank — Pueblo — Sioux — Navajo

S + [crayon BLUE] - BL
The __Sioux__ Indians lived in tepees made of buffalo hides.

[knot] - T + V + [arrow up] - P + [axe]
The __Navajo__ Indians lived in hogans made of wood and straw.

P + [web] + [SLOW sign] - S
The __Pueblo__ Indians lived in adobes made of earth.

174

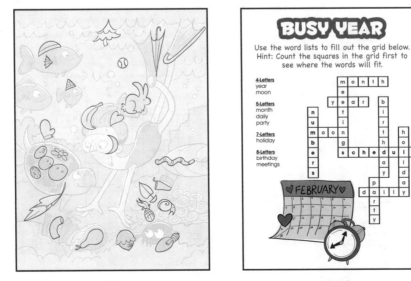

176 — BUSY YEAR

Use the word lists to fill out the grid below.
Hint: Count the squares in the grid first to see where the words will fit.

4-Letters
year
moon

5-Letters
month
daily
party

7-Letters
holiday

8-Letters
birthday
meetings

Answer Key

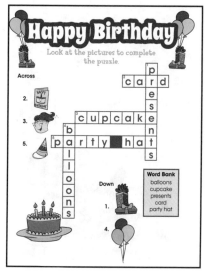

177

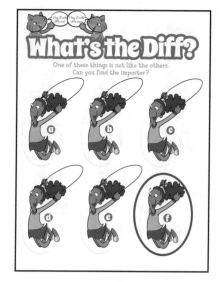

178

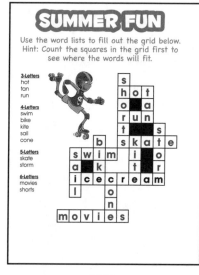

179

180

182

360

Answer Key

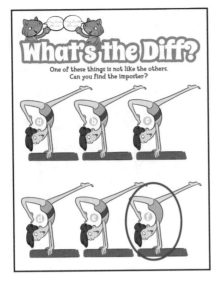

183

184

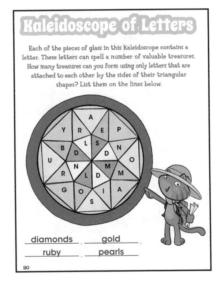

186

187

188

Answer Key

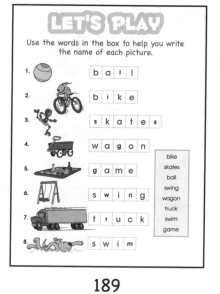

189

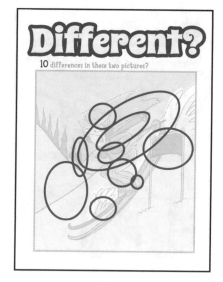

191

192

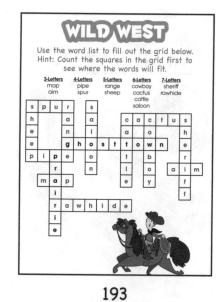

193

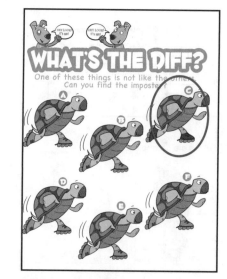

194

362

Answer Key

195

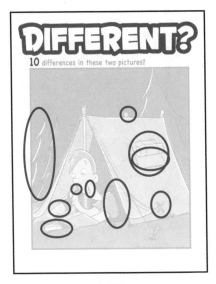

197

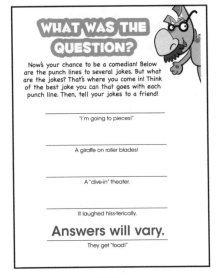

199

200

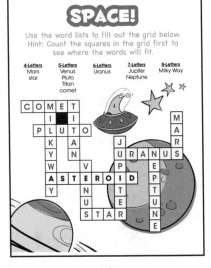

201

Answer Key

202

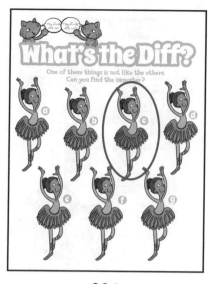

204

205

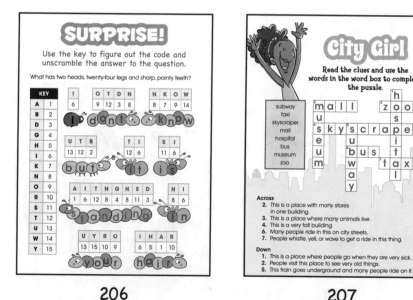

206

207

364

Answer Key

209

210

211

212

214

Answer Key

RHYME THIS!

Using the pictures as hints, fill in the missing letters of the rhyming words.

G U M
D R U M

S N A K E
C A K E

K I T E
B I T E

215

Glamorous Glasses

Add a vowel to each word below to make a new word Gladys can see through her glasses.

Gladys has some goofy glasses. They have springs on them which stretch out words to make room for more vowels.

p i n k   p u r p l e
f r a m e   s p e c s
g e e k   c a t e y e

216

DOUBLE DUTY

Homographs are words that have the same spellings but have different meanings and often different pronunciations. Use the clues to find the missing homographs.

Watch the clam **close** its shell **close** to the clownfish.
(shut)   (near)

The prickly porcupine will **present** the **present** to the patient prairie dog.
(give)   (gift)

I **wound** the **wound** of the whimpering wolf with white gauze.
(wrapped around)   (cut)

I will **project** a **project** for providing the polar bear with polka-dotted pajamas.
(predict)   (plan)

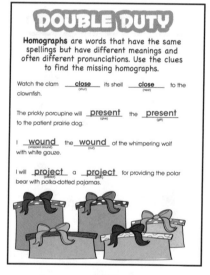

217

218

Alike but Different

Write titles for these paintings. The first one has been done for you. Then, draw your own painting and write a title for it.

a hare with hair   a pair   a knight
                     of pears   at night

a flower   Drawings will vary.
in the flour   Answers will vary.

220

Answer Key

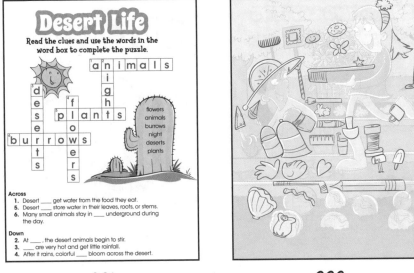

221

222

224

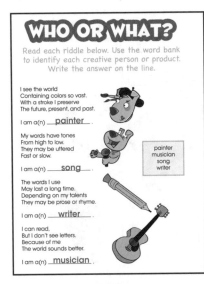

225

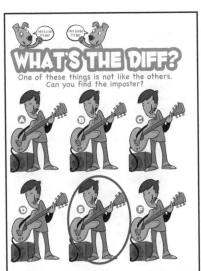

226

Answer Key

SHARE TWO LETTERS

Each word has two letters in common with the other words. Using the pictures as hints, fill in the rest of the words.

1. D O O R
2. C O R E
3. S N O R E
4. G O R I L L A
5. H O R S E
6. H O R N
7. F O R K

227

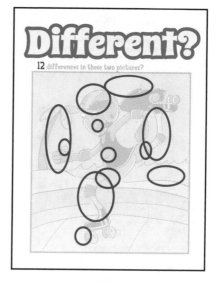

Different?

12 differences in these two pictures?

229

ANIMAL ANALOGIES

Use the word bank to help complete these analogies. An analogy is the expression of two like comparisons.

rattlesnake	cow	camel	elephant

A **hill** is to **land** as a **hump** is to a(n) **camel**.

A **hand fan** is to a **human** as **ears** are to a(n) **elephant**.

Four quarters are to a **dollar** as **four stomachs** are to a(n) **COW**.

A **chest beat** is to a **gorilla** as a **shaking rattle** is to a(n) **rattlesnake**.

230

Instrument Chatter

Use the word bank to help solve each riddle about musical instruments.

In my triangle-shaped body
Many strings have I.
The notes I play
Are from low to high.

I am a(n) **harp**

High sounds you'll hear
When you play me.
A long tube with holes
Is what you'll see.

I am a(n) **flute**

Strum my strings
And sing in a band.
I play rock and roll
In a way so grand!

I am a(n) **guitar**

You'll hear a bang
When you hit my top.
Once you hit me,
It's hard to stop.

I am a(n) **drum**

Deep sounds you'll hear
When you play me.
Lots of shiny, bright brass
Is what you'll see.

I am a(n) **tuba**

guitar
flute
tuba
harp
drum

231

RHYME THIS!

Using the pictures as hints, fill in the missing letters of the rhyming words.

F I S H
D I S H

K N E E
T R E E

R O A C H
C O A C H

232

Answer Key

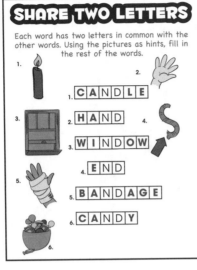

233

234

236

MYSTERY PICTURE

Read each sentence and cross out the picture.
What picture is left?

1. It is not a toy.
2. It is not foil.
3. It is not boil.
4. It is not coins.
5. It is not soil.
6. It is not oil.

The mystery picture is a _____ boy _____

237

238

369

Answer Key

Forest Life

Read the sentences and use the words in the word box to complete the puzzle.

		²s				
⁴f	o	r	e	s	t	
³s	q	u	i	r	r	e	l	s

(crossword puzzle with answers: sunlight, forest, squirrels, deer, insects, trees)

Word box:
sunlight   trees
forest   squirrels
insects   deer

Across
3. ____ climb trees and eat acorns.
5. Many ____ crawl along the forest floor.
6. Many ____ grow in the forest.

Down
1. A little bit of ____ shines through the trees.
2. It is cool and dark in the ____ .
4. A ____ nibbles on the sweet green plants.

239

240

RHYME TIME

Using the pictures as hints, fill in the missing letters of the rhyming words.

S	U	N
R	U	N

B	O	N	E
P	H	O	N	E

C	O	R	N
H	O	R	N

242

Nursery Rhymes

Read the clues and use the words in the word box to complete the puzzle.

Word box:
clock
lamb
hill
sheep
shoe
fiddle
horn
corner

(crossword puzzle with answers: hill, fiddle, lamb, shoe, sheep, clock, horn, corner)

Across
2. Jack and Jill went up the ____.
4. One, two, buckle my ____.
7. Little Jack Horner sat in the ____.

Down
1. Hey diddle, diddle, the cat and the ____.
3. Mary had a little ____.
4. Little Bo-peep has lost her ____.
5. Hickory, dickory, dock, the mouse ran up the ____.
6. Little Boy Blue, come blow your ____.

243

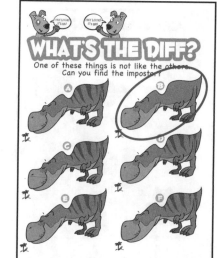

WHAT'S THE DIFF?

One of these things is not like the others. Can you find the imposter?

244

370

Answer Key

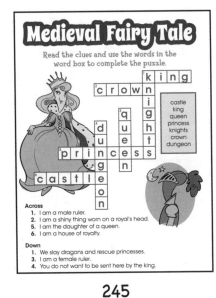

Medieval Fairy Tale

Read the clues and use the words in the word box to complete the puzzle.

```
            ¹k i n g
      ²c r o w n
            i
         ³q g
         u h
      ⁴d u e e n
      u  ⁵p r i n c e s s
      n  n
      ⁶c a s t l e
      e
      o
      n
```

Word box: castle, king, queen, princess, knights, crown, dungeon

Across
1. I am a male ruler.
2. I am a shiny thing worn on a royal's head.
5. I am the daughter of a queen.
6. I am a house of royalty.

Down
1. We slay dragons and rescue princesses.
3. I am a female ruler.
4. You do not want to be sent here by the king.

245

WHAT'S THE DIFF?

One of these things is not like the others. Can you find the imposter?

246

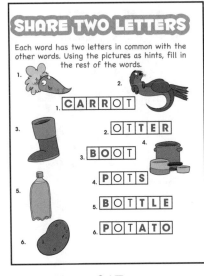

SHARE TWO LETTERS

Each word has two letters in common with the other words. Using the pictures as hints, fill in the rest of the words.

1. C A R R O T
2. O T T E R
3. B O O T
4. P O T S
5. B O T T L E
6. P O T A T O

247

WHAT'S THE DIFF?

One of these things is not like the others. Can you find the imposter?

248

What a Great Place!

Fill in the puzzle with words that name the pictures below. Use the word box to help you.

1. e r a s e r
2. t e a c h e r
3. c h a l k
4. c r a y o n s
5. b o o k
6. p e n c i l

Word box: teacher, pencil, book, crayons, eraser, chalk

The letters in the circles going down spell a mystery word. The word names a place where all these things can be found. Write the mystery word.

school

249

371

Answer Key

251

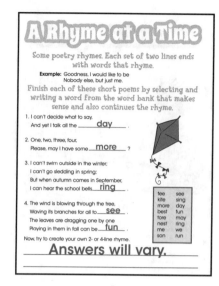

252

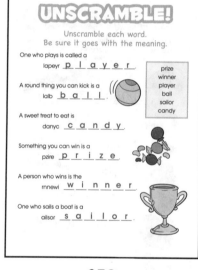

253

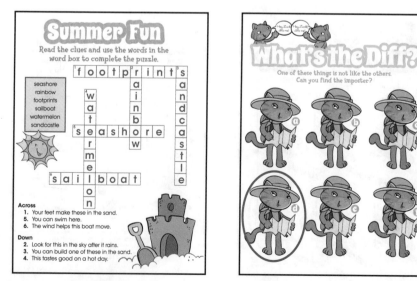

254   255

Answer Key

256

One Becomes Two

Think of a word that could be the last part of
one compound word and the first part of a
different compound word. Write the missing word
to make two different compound words.

pea __nut__ cracker   cat __fish__ bowl

sun __flower__ pot   sea __shell__ fish

cook __book__ worm   bob __cat__ tail

doll __house__ fly   bird __bath__ tub

cat	nut	flower	shell
book	fish	bath	house

Think of another compound word and draw a picture for it.

Drawings will vary.

258

GRAND CANYON

Complete each fact about the Grand Canyon
by unscrambling the letters at the end of
each sentence. Use the word bank
if necessary.

Mead	desert	Colorado
Arizona	deep	

The canyon is between 4,000 and 5,000 feet __deep__ .
(epde)

The Grand Canyon is located in northwestern __Arizona__ .
(zanioar)

The canyon was formed by the __Colorado__ River. (rodoclao)

The bottom of the Grand Canyon is mostly __desert__ .
(seetrd)

The lake that forms at the southern end of the Grand Canyon is
called Lake __Mead__ . (deam)

What kind of animals do you think live in the Grand Canyon?
Draw a picture of one.

Drawings will vary.

259

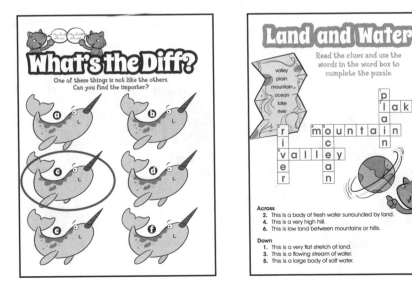

What's the Diff?

One of these things is not like the others.
Can you find the imposter?

260

Land and Water

Read the clues and use the
words in the word box to
complete the puzzle.

valley
plain
mountain
ocean
lake
river

Across
2. This is a body of fresh water surrounded by land.
4. This is a very high hill.
6. This is low land between mountains or hills.

Down
1. This is a very flat stretch of land.
3. This is a flowing stream of water.
5. This is a large body of salt water.

261

Answer Key

263

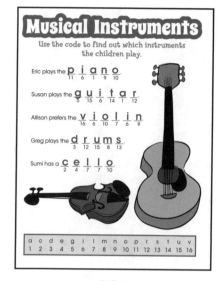

264

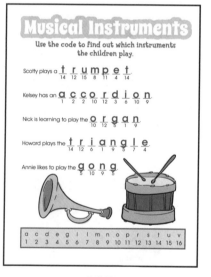

265

266   267

374

Answer Key

268

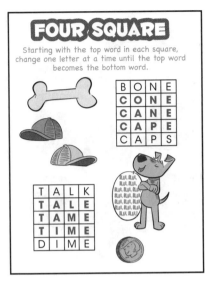

269

270

272

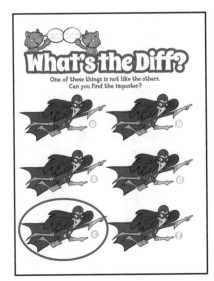

273

Answer Key

274

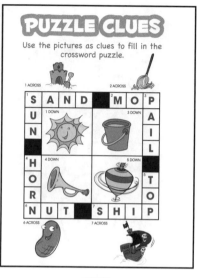

275

276

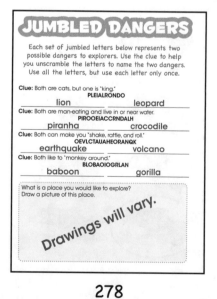

278

279

Answer Key

280

281

282

284

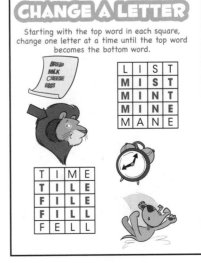

285

Answer Key

286

287

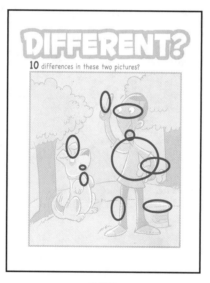

289

290

291

Answer Key

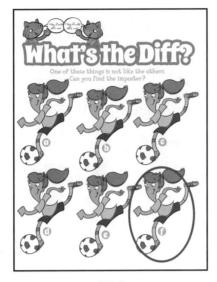

292

293

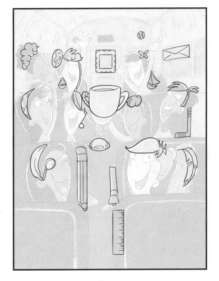

294

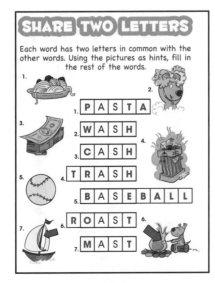

296

297

Answer Key

298

300

301

302

303

380

Answer Key

305

306

307

308

309

310

Answer Key

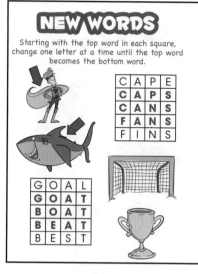

311

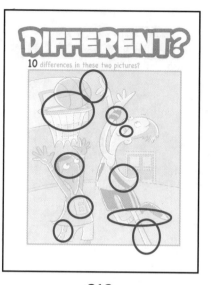

313

314

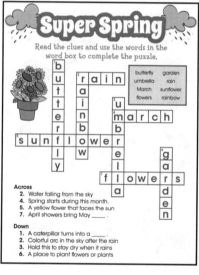

315

316

318